AN INTRODUCTION TO
HINDUSTANI CLASSICAL MUSIC

OTHER LOTUS TITLES

FORTHCOMING TITLES

An Introduction To

HINDUSTANI CLASSICAL MUSIC

A GUIDEBOOK FOR BEGINNERS

Vijay Prakash Singha

Foreword by
Shyam Benegal

LOTUS COLLECTION
ROLI BOOKS

Lotus Collection

© Vijay Prakash Singha, 2014

First published in 2014

The Lotus Collection
An imprint of
Roli Books Pvt. Ltd
M-75, Greater Kailash II Market, New Delhi 110 048
Phone: ++91 (011) 40682000
Fax: ++91 (011) 2921 7185
E-mail: info@rolibooks.com
Website: www.rolibooks.com
Also at Bengaluru, Chennai, & Mumbai

Cover Design: Qualcom Designs
Layout: Sanjeev Mathpal
Production: Shaji Sahadevan

ISBN: 978-81-7436-919-2

Typeset in Cochin LT Std by Roli Books Pvt. Ltd.
Printed at Devtech Printers Pvt Ltd.

Contents

For Devika, a budding
musician herself

Foreword

Of all the arts, music is the most abstract and by far the most evocative; emotionally, cerebrally and as some might claim, spiritually.

There is nothing quite like a piece of music of any genre to take you into a moodspace of its choosing. Whether it is light music like bhajans or film songs, or music set to compulsive rhythms such as Rock, Hip Hop, Be Bop, or compellingly improvisatory as Jazz, Blues or Folk from different parts of the world, or classically derived musical compositions from across the planet, music transports you through a range of emotions and feelings, often difficult to describe. Music can make your heart beat faster, blood course more vigorously or conversely sail you into an ocean of calm and tranquility.

Unlike most countries of the world, India is heir to some of the most diverse forms of music; classical, folk, and contemporary. It is an abundance of riches with a vast array of folk-forms and an exceptionally sophisticated classical lexicon.

India has two classical traditions each with its own distinct character yet closely allied to one another – Hindustani, meaning North Indian and Carnatic, representing the traditions of the South. Hindustani classical music ranges all the way from spiritual and religious to secular and profane. There are a myriad musical forms like thumris, dadras, kajris at one end of the spectrum to elaborate renditions of ragas in dhrupad and khayal forms. Each raga is a set of notes in a given order that gives the raga a specific and particular melodic character. The singer or the instrumentalist takes the raga or mode as the basis for musical elaboration which corresponds in many ways to an exciting and serendipitous musical journey into the known and unknown, the familiar and the new.

Hindustani classical music is a highly evolved form that has ragas corresponding to different times of the day from dawn to dusk and through the night. Then again there are ragas that express the unique character of each season.

Unlike Western classical music which took the route of harmonies and counterpoint after the introduction of polyphony, Hindustani classical music is firmly tied to melody.

The aesthetic under-pinning of Indian classical music is based on an aesthetic theory that goes back more than sixteen hundred years – the Rasa theory, originally applied to the performing arts in the treatise *Natya Shastra* by Bharata. The author elaborated on what constitutes aesthetic experience in Art. He enumerated the basic human emotions as being nine in number.

Sringara: love and longing

Hasya: funny, amusing and unexpected

Karuna: compassion

Raudra: fury and anger

Veer: heroic

Vibhatsa: disgust

Bhayanaka: terrifying

Adbhuta: wonder

Shanta: tranquility, calm and repose

In life, experience of these emotions is real and therefore stable. In an artistic work emotion is savoured rather than experienced. What is savoured, is the essence of the emotion. It is fleeting and unstable and lasts only as long as one is exposed to the work of art. More than any other art form, the appreciation and experience of Indian classical music corresponds most easily and directly to the Rasa theory.

Sadly, not many books have been written for the lay person to help appreciate and savour Hindustani classical music.

A welcome addition to the few books that exist is Vijay Prakash Singha's comprehensive and uncomplicated introduction to Hindustani classical music which he calls a guidebook for beginners. It is simply written, cogent in its explanation, and will go a long way in making even a casual listener into a *rasik*.

Shyam Benegal

Introduction

Whenever we meet people familiar with Hindustani classical music, a little digging usually reveals that this familiarity is 'received knowledge' from parents, teachers, or from somebody they admired or respected as youngsters. Seldom, if ever, have they acquired it themselves. What about the many others who may be genuinely interested in learning about such music, but had no one to share their knowledge with them? How can they acquire some of it on their own? Where should they turn for guidance? A cursory survey of the market reveals that there is hardly any self-help material available to guide a beginner. Whatever there is on the bookshelves is useful only to those who already have a working knowledge of the subject. There is very little, indeed, for the novice. The greenhorn, rather than finding his way into the enchanted world of Hindustani classical music, is likely to lose it altogether. Worse, he may never come back for fear of getting lost again.

This guidebook is an effort to bridge this gap. It is written specially for novices, by a listener like themselves, who might be a bit more experienced, but is a listener all the same. I am neither a musician nor a musicologist, but an avid listener who, after many years of listening has been transformed into a *rasik*. A *rasik* is one who has savoured a flower's nectar or *ras* and become addicted to it. A *rasik* is an 'informed listener.' Unlike a glass of wine, which is soon gone, the *rasik's* glass gets full every time he sips from it.

People unfamiliar with Indian classical music are often hesitant to take up listening to it because they feel that either they are too obtuse for such heavy stuff, or that it is too abstruse for them. Still others are wary of being thought dilettantes. I hope to alleviate such unfounded beliefs, and assure readers that Hindustani classical music is well within the reach of anyone who desires to learn to appreciate it, irrespective of their complete lack of any prior knowledge.

This guidebook has been written with a view to helping beginners become *rasiks*.

References to famous musicians from the past might appear dated in a contemporary guidebook, but it must be remembered that in all classical genres, a century or two is not the same thing as it is in their popular counterparts. Till the genre is alive, musicians who practised it are also part of living memory. The skill and expertise they have bequeathed to their succeeding generations continue to be a source of joy and wonderment long after they have shed their mortal coil. This is why we still read the poetry of Mirza Ghalib and the literary works of William Shakespeare. Merely listing out the names of great maestros, past and present, would hardly be of any help. Thus, while explaining the significance of the gharana system of Hindustani classical music, I have made a mention of the better-known musicians belonging to each gharana.

In the world of Hindustani classical music, its practitioners have traditionally been addressed by various appellations: A Hindu male practitioner who has high achievements to his name is addressed as Pandit. Similarly, a Muslim male practitioner is called Ustad. Among Hindu females, *Devi* is suffixed after their names, for example Siddheshwari Devi, whereas among Muslim ladies, the appellation Begum is added, either as a prefix or suffix, for example Begum Akhtar or Roshanara Begum. In Maharashtra, the practice of suffixing the term Bai after the name of female musicians is in vogue, such as Kesarbai Kerkar. Of late, the prefix Vidushi is also gaining currency, which, in Sanskrit, means a learned woman.

Historical events that occurred during the development of Hindustani classical music over the centuries have been dealt with in a fair amount of detail. It is essential for beginners to understand the relevance of each age and stage that this music has passed through in its evolution, from ancient times to the present day. An accurate account of the circumstances under which various musical instruments evolved into their current shape and form helps clear the myths of antiquity, that might cloud reality. The art of Hindustani classical music is an ancient one, but not everything else associated with it belongs to antiquity. Many facets considered an inseparable part of it today were outside its pale in the past, and have merged into it over the years.

For example, the saraswati veena, associated with the Goddess of Learning, has been around from the beginning of music in India, while the tabla is just over two centuries old. As per Indian/Hindu mythology, the flute has been played by cowherds since the time of Lord Krishna, but it took a genius like Pandit Pannalal Ghosh to transform it from a folk to a classical instrument just over half a century ago. A device of unmatched musical precision, the sarangi, dates back to Ravan, the mythical King of Lanka in the Hindu epic, Ramayana. South Indian musicians borrowed the violin from Western classical music just two hundred years ago and made it an integral part of Carnatic sangeet, whereas Pandit Vishwa Mohan Bhatt reincarnated the Hawaiian guitar as the mohan veena and won an Emmy award for it only a decade ago.

Music recitals today differ vastly, and for the better, from the time when the Indian recording industry came into being a hundred years ago. In those days, the tabla player was no more than an adjunct, a mere timekeeper who played standing on one side of the stage, with the tablas strung in a hammock around his neck. Today, he is an equal partner, seated alongside the main artiste, whom he occasionally even overshadows on the stage. A hundred years ago, the santoor did not exist in the classical firmament and the sarod was but a shadow of what it is today. An informed listener should be aware of these historical developments to achieve a holistic understanding of the subject.

An over-emphasis on the technical configuration of various ragas, their leading musical notes (*vadi / samvadi swar*) and so on, is something that scares off the beginner. Such instruction is mandatory for, and intrinsic to, the syllabus of a student who is training as a musician. There is really no need to burden an uninitiated beginner with such minutiae, when all he wants to do is to become an informed listener. In the beginning, it should matter little if he is not able to critically analyze a raga.

In the course of time, he will develop the ability to do so, and if he is a true seeker, will be able to unearth whatever he needs to know about his favourite ragas on his own.

Almost three-quarters of Hindi and regional film songs are based on ragas. Yet, how many film music buffs truly know which ragas their favourite numbers are based on? As the beginner proceeds on his journey, he will acquire a fondness for some ragas over others and will eventually learn to identify them by their underlying characteristics. For this reason, neither does this book dwell too much on this aspect of ragas, nor does it call upon the beginner to do so right at the start. He is encouraged to seek out such information of his own volition, which is what 'informed' listening is all about.

Listening and learning is the best way for a beginner to become an informed listener. Beginning with simpler, easier to comprehend musical modes, the novice should graduate to higher levels. To this end, a list of recommended listening is given separately. Similarly, reading and self-education increase our understanding and ability to appreciate classical music. A suggested reading list is also included. The association of classical music with Hindi films has also been examined, to highlight the profound influence of the former on the latter. The future of Indian classical music has been discussed to prepare young listeners for what the twenty-first century is likely to unfold.

1

A Unique Creation of the Human Mind

According to legend, when Brahma, the creator deity, created the *Brahmand* (cosmos), there was nothing but sound (*naad*). Ancient Indians categorized sound as struck and unstruck. *Naad Brahma* is a philosophical concept that signifies the primordial, unstruck sound from which all other sounds are believed to ensue. In yogic practice, this is called *anahat naad* (unstruck sound), which is reportedly heard when the spirit merges with the Absolute (Brahman). All other sound is called *aahat naad* (struck sound), created by the collision of, or the friction between, two objects. According to Matang Muni, a seventh century music commentator, *swar* (musical note) is a sound that glows on its own – *swa* means self, and *ra* means *rajari*, luminous. He argued that if a physical entity like phosphorus can glow on its own, why could another physical entity, like sound, not do the same? Indians thus associate sound and, by extension, music, with the divine.

When George Harrison, one of the Beatles, came to India to study Hindustani classical music with Pandit Ravi Shankar, his teacher started him off with the age-old Indian concept of *Naad Brahma*. After his first few lessons, Harrison is said to have remarked, 'Indian classical music is light years ahead of the music of the West.' Despite this tribute from a musician of international repute, our music rarely finds mention in the ancient, medieval, and modern history of India. In contrast, innumerable tomes have been written on the history of Western classical music, its composers and musicians, their orchestras and conductors. The only historian of repute to have dwelt on the music of India is the noted Indologist, Prof A.L. Basham, in his magnum opus, *The Wonder that was India*. He not only describes the music in some technical detail, but also comments on its antecedents that date back to about 1500 BCE. Other noted historians, including several Indians, have left the subject alone.

Music is believed to be the highest form of human artistic endeavour. The great saint-philosopher of modern India, Swami Vivekananda (1863-1902), said, 'Music is the highest art, and to those who understand it, the highest worship.' We can neither see it nor touch it, yet it engenders such a variety of emotions in our hearts and minds. So many theses have been written on the effects of music, ranging from the mundane to the metaphysical, that there is no denying its universal influence on mankind since the beginning of time. Music is one of the oldest arts and took root in all cultures and civilizations as they flourished and sought to reach their highest potential. Over millennia, however, only two ancient musical traditions have survived the ravages of time and gone on to achieve the sophistication of 'high art'. Western classical music is one, and its Indian counterpart, the other.

THE BEGINNER'S DILEMMA

The beginner interested in learning more about this vital facet of Indian culture, which appears to be a cloistered world of its own, is faced with considerable difficulties. Almost all available books on Indian classical music have been written by erudite pundits and in scholarly language, which deter the novice. Lecture-demonstrations (lec-dems) and appreciation albums have the same drawback. There is too much musical grammar, scholastic distraction and technical minutiae, which weigh down the novice embarking upon what should be a pleasurable journey of discovery.

It would, however, be unfair to blame musicologists writing such books, or scholar-musicians making appreciation albums, as they are sincerely and wholeheartedly attempting to further the cause of an art that they hold dear. It is because they have so much knowledge and experience at their disposal that they are unable to gauge just how much a novice can absorb, and how much can be left for him to find out for himself later.

Spic-Macay (Society for the Propagation of Indian Classical Music and Culture Amongst Youth) deserves an honourable mention here. Although they have generated considerable awareness about Indian classical music in schools and colleges, they have been trying to popularize it among the youth in general, rather than making it accessible to those who come to it of their own volition. Hindustani classical music is not meant to be popular. No classical system is, in any discipline, anywhere in the world. Such systems follow long-established traditions of classical antiquity, and are intended to be of permanent, rather than ephemeral value. They are sought after only by those who have an aesthetically sensitive and cerebrally developed bent of mind. The aim must be to render music comprehensible to those who seek it, as opposed to turning it into a form with mass-based appeal.

After discarding excess baggage from any tradition, what is left is its core, its essence. The core of Indian classical music has three constituents. First, the history of its evolution from the earliest times to the present. Second, what we call 'the feel' of the tradition, its *ras-bhav* (mood-emotion). And third, 'the need to know principle', that is, how much a learner ought to know at the start and how much can be left to him to pursue later. A familiar stumbling block in this quest is the view of some eminent musicologists that 'Indian classical music cannot be explained'. This implies that it is impossible to literally express, in words, its emotional and cultural content with the exactitude and accuracy that the aural guild tradition demands.

Fortunately, this is not as bad as it sounds. What these scholars mean is that the music is so thoroughly intertwined with its cultural ambience that it goes beyond the realm of analyses in theoretically exact terms. This is usually meant vis-a-vis Western classical music, which can withstand such analyses. Indian classical music speaks directly from, and to, the heart – the hearts of the guru (teacher) and his shishya (pupil.) Its past is so intimately enmeshed in the history and culture of this ancient land that it is imperative that these aspects too, are thoroughly grasped before its artistic beauty can be fully imbibed in the contemporary context.

To cite an example, we might examine the universal popularity of American 'country music'. The cowboy, his ranch and the prairie have long appealed to young people everywhere. They have loved 'Westerns' ever since cinema began, and fondly listened to the songs of Johnny Cash, Hank Locklin, and John Denver without ever leaving their hometowns halfway across the globe. This is because they were able to identify with the milieu of the movies, their music, and the places, however faraway they might have been. This analogy might seem far-fetched, but the underlying sentiment is close enough to make the point. In other words, the student must be able to imbibe the underlying socio-historical realities of the host country in order to appreciate the culture that blossomed within it.

Pandit Ravi Shankar has gone on record to support the theory that Indian classical music cannot be taught like any other subject. Its feel is incomprehensible unless its milieu is experienced personally, no matter how learned the teacher or how bright the pupil. This can be achieved only when the student is brought in contact with the Indian ethos, whereby he acquires this knowledge as a *sanskar*, a cultural refinement. That is why it is recommended that a formal student of Indian classical music, even one who is born in India, should live and study in an ashram, an academy, or the home of his teacher. That is where he picks up the *sanskars* that help him imbibe the tradition in its entirety.

Whenever scholars have attempted to explain this music theoretically, they have unwittingly created scholastic webs that cannot be penetrated by the beginner. Does this, therefore, mean that one can gain an insight into this enchanted world only by joining an ashram? The answer is two-fold: We do not want to initiate the beginner into musical scholarship and virtuosity, but we do want him to become an informed and appreciative listener. This is the 'need to know' principle as it applies to a beginner. And that brings us to the aim of this guidebook: A beginner cannot, and need not, become a virtuoso, but he can certainly become an informed listener. A *rasik*, the culturally correct term for such a listener, is a lover of music and the arts – an aesthete. This differentiates him from the *vidwaan* (scholar), or *shastri* (teacher).

ORIGINS: THE AURAL GUILD TRADITION

An important aspect that should be highlighted right at the beginning is the unique process by which this music has been kept alive over the centuries. This is the aural guild tradition, referred to as the guru-shishya parampara (the 'teacher-student tradition'). Whatever formal organization that we see in it today by way of codification, notation, and so on, has occurred only in the twentieth century. Before that, it was handed down from generation to generation, from father to son and from teacher to pupil, by word of mouth. In contrast, Western classical music was codified and notated right from its inception.

The classical music of India is over three thousand years old. It has had a fascinating past, through the cycle of ages. Among the arts and sciences the ancient Indo-Aryans indulged in, music occupied a prominent place. In the beginning, it was essentially a *shastric* music performed by the priestly class. The term *shastric* connotes the classical, *shastra* being the Sanskrit word for scripture. One who was learned in the *shastras* was known as a *shastri*. This is the reason Indian classical music is called *shastriya* sangeet. In ancient times, it was closely interlinked with the faith and traditions of its people

There is a prevalent belief today that the younger generations have turned away from their cultural traditions in India. This view does not take into account the momentous transformation that India underwent in the nineteenth and twentieth centuries, from a feudal, agrarian society to an egalitarian, semi-industrial one. It is a transition that has touched every walk of life, and brought with it more change in the last 100 years than in the preceding 500 years. Classical music along with many of our indigenous arts and crafts has also suffered the vagaries of rapid transformation and modernization.

India's youth should have been the rightful custodians of a magnificent musical heritage, of which they are heirs. However, for a variety of reasons, including Lord Thomas Babington Macaulay's famous 'minute' of the 1830s on English education for the natives, it seems to have gone out of their reach, remaining restricted to that section of society where it has been traditionally taught, practised, and performed: the *gullies* and *mohallas* of Lucknow, Benaras, and Old Delhi. This ghettoization has prevented genuine music lovers from outside this fraternity from participating in the tradition. Somewhere along the way, that section of society that was the purveyor of this ancient tradition, got left behind, even as society as a whole moved on, creating a chasm of incomprehension between the two. This has been further widened by the insular orthodoxy of the former and the liberal modernity of the latter.

In fact, if the educated elite of India itself were alienated from its classical music, what chance was there of the latter reaching foreign shores? It was only in 1955, when Yehudi (later Lord) Menuhin, the greatest Western violinist of modern times, took Ali Akbar Khan and his sarod to America that international audiences got a chance to learn about this ancient musical tradition. Lord Menuhin did the same thing with Ali Akbar's brother-in-law, Ravi Shankar and his sitar the next year. Accompanying these two instrumentalists were the legendary percussionists, first Kanhai Dutta, and later, Allah Rakha, who showed to the world the unfathomable intricacies of the ancient rhythm cycles of the Indian drum, the tabla.

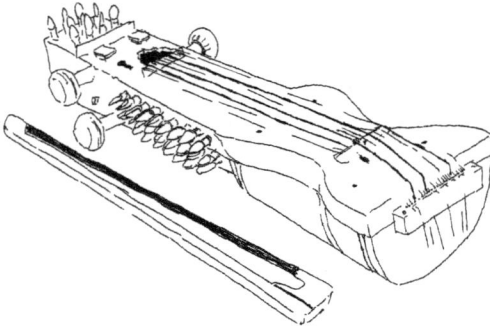

2

Understanding Hindustani Classical Music

The term 'Indian classical music' encompasses the two main schools of classical music in the subcontinent – the northern and the southern. In the course of time, the music of north India came to be called 'Hindustani', and that of the south, 'Carnatic'. This book concerns the former, that is, Hindustani classical music.

Like all music, the music of India is also based on the twelve-note scale of seven 'pure' or *shuddha* notes (*Sa, Re, Ga, Ma, Pa, Dha, Ni*), and five flat, or *komal*, and sharp or *teevra* notes. In Western music, both the lower and upper *sa* are counted, making a total of eight pure notes. These eight notes comprise an 'Octave'. In the Indian system, only the first *sa* is counted and the seven notes constitute a *Saptak* (like the latin *septet*). Besides musical notes, the other two pillars that hold up the edifice of music are rhythm and tempo. All three aspects, as they are incorporated in Indian classical music, have been explained to the extent that a beginner needs to know and the author's knowledge permits.

Beginners should learn about the birth of Hindustani classical music and the cultural ethos within which it developed over millennia. *Ras-bhav*, the emotional 'feel' of the music, also needs to be understood, since it lies at the core of the *rasik's* aesthetic experience. During its long journey, Hindustani classical music was confined to the human voice. Vocal music remained predominant till the age of Tansen (1506-1589). It was only in the eighteenth and nineteenth centuries that musical instruments which have become an integral part of it today, came to the fore. As instrumental music became popular, listeners started classifying the two as vocal and instrumental. In reality, there is no such classification and both vocal and instrumental music form part of a monolithic whole, called Hindustani classical music. This concept is clarified if we understand that Pandit Ravi Shankar is not just a sitarist but a Hindustani classical musician, who produces music on the sitar.

A *rasik* should also have a comprehensive understanding of the basics of a Hindustani classical music recital in terms of its architecture, format, and movements. Beginners must know what going to a concert entails, and how they can enjoy a recital to the fullest. For this, they should be familiar with percussion instruments and have a working knowledge of rhythm and tempo.

The global success of Indians in technology and commerce is well known, as are their achievements in literature, films, and the fine arts. Matching achievements in classical music, however, have been few and far between. This has led to a decline in listeners. One wonders if there are still any seekers left, and if so, where are they? They may not be readily visible, but if we look closely, we will find them all around us, at home as well as among the diaspora, keen to know what lies at the heart of this music and how they can enjoy its timeless beauty. Equally keen are a growing number of foreign seekers, some of whom even come to India to learn more about Indian classical music.

There is a Sanskrit saying that those who seek sincerely will surely find their teacher. The guru will appear when the pupil is ready. I went to a boarding school where our English headmaster insisted on giving us a taste of our own culture. Morning assembly began with a Sanskrit prayer and ended with a 78 rpm record of Western and Hindustani classical music on alternate days, played on an amplified gramophone. It was compulsory for boys from standards five to eight to attend a Hindustani classical music class once a week, which became optional from the ninth standard.

Having opted to continue with the class, by the age of sixteen, I became equally familiar with Beethoven and Mozart as with Pannalal Ghosh and Bismillah Khan. What I did not realize was the value of what I had learnt. This dawned on me only as a college fresher, when some senior 'culture-vultures' took me along to a sitar recital by Ustad Vilayat Khan at Vigyan Bhawan in New Delhi. It was the first live concert I had attended, and, for a small-town boy, it was a most memorable experience. As it got underway, I noticed that most of the seniors were not really familiar with what they were hearing and seemed to have gone simply because it was expected of them. On the other hand, I was able to follow the recital in detail, from start to finish. This not only enhanced my status but also elicited an invitation from the girls' college across the road to attend their music appreciation seminar. All this came simply because an English headmaster had drilled something invaluable into the head of a young schoolboy. Ever since, I have felt myself uniquely privileged, as if I were a member of an exclusive club.

History tells us that throughout the ages and across civilizations, a rarified exclusivity has been associated with the classical arts in general, and with music in particular. It is an accepted practice in historiography to evaluate the worth of a civilization by examining the highest point, the acme, of its socio-cultural achievement, and not the lowest point, the nadir, of its degeneration. Another widely-held view, substantiated by Pandit Birju Maharaj, kathak dancer par excellence, thumri singer, percussionist, painter, and composer, in an interview to Mrinal Pande on her programme *Baaton Baaton Mein* on Lok Sabha TV, is that 'there is no democracy in the arts and artistic talent is not distributed equally'. We may add that this lack of democracy extends to the appreciators of the arts as well. A *rasik* may thus well have a hint of justifiable cultural snobbery in his self-image.

Everyone cannot become a *rasik*. I feel that classical music aficionados everywhere are a class by themselves, and a class apart. Within this 'class', however, there are no princes or paupers. All are seekers of the one true light. There is no telling when and where one might bump into another of one's own kind. It might be at a well-attended concert in a glittering auditorium, or at an intimate baithak in the humble home of a penurious practitioner. For instance, the first music teacher of twelve-year-old Bhimsen Joshi was Agasara Chennappa, the village dhobi in Gagad district, Karnataka. Seventy-four years later, Bhimsen was honoured with India's highest award, the Bharat Ratna, in 2008, but he never forgot his first teacher and continued to retain fond memories of him.

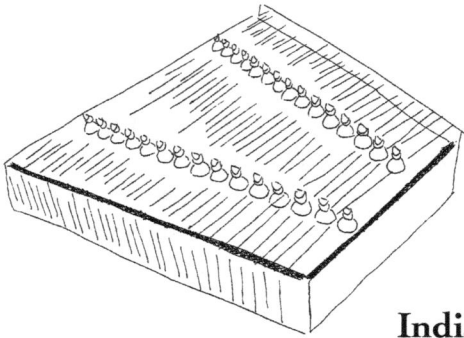

3

Birth and Development of Indian Classical Music

The music of India is so intimately intertwined with its culture that it is impossible to understand one without a proper grounding in the other. It is like gazing at the Taj Mahal without giving a thought to its foundation. One cannot get the feel of the music without first experiencing the 'idea of India'. Indian culture is a kaleidoscope that has often been viewed through the prism of its spiritual philosophy. The term 'religion' is as inadequate to describe this philosophy as is the term 'Hinduism' while referring to Sanatan Dharma, the 'eternal path of righteous living' that the people of India, of all religions, strive to follow, notwithstanding the failure of the nation-state to do so on many counts.

It is as important for the Indian alienated from his roots as it is for a foreigner to get a feel of the Indian mind. This may be attempted at two planes – the natural (*prakriti*, the field of matter) and the human (*purush*, intellectual consciousness). Central to our physical world, and which regulates nature in all its manifestations, is the sun. A prayer to the sun is, therefore, the most sacred of all hymns in India's oldest scripture, the Rig Veda. This is the Gayatri Mantra, which makes humanity aware of its oneness with the cosmos. As human beings, we must understand this oneness, which also underlies the *rasik's* aesthetic experience.

The music of India is an extension of this philosophy. Pandit Ravi Shankar's autobiography, *My Music, My Life* tells us more about the intimate correlation of the culture of India with its music. He recalls his time in Baba Allauddin Khan's ashram at Maihar in Central India, where he stayed, did all the household chores and learnt from his guru, not only how to play the sitar, but all about the basic principles of Hindustani classical music, its ancient history and cultural traditions. In fact, it is one of the finest written accounts describing the guru-shishya tradition by one who actually lived it.

NAVARASA AND THE MUSES

Natural phenomena have diverse effects on human beings, whose mental reactions to each phenomenon are equally varied. These reactions have led philosophers to speculate on the spectrum of emotions that comprise the human mind. The thinkers of ancient India concluded that these emotions were nine in number, and called them navarasa, or the 'nine mood-emotions'.

Among the nine rasas that Shyam Benegal has enumerated in his Foreword to this book, the one listed first, *Shringar rasa*, is of foremost importance to the *rasik* of Hindustani classical music. It is an aesthetic perception and not the emotional experience alone that an informed listener undergoes when he enjoys good music. Shringar rasa encompasses all the 'perceptions of love' that lie at the heart of this music, be it the devotional love of a worshipper towards his Creator, as in the entire canon of *Raas-Leela*, the love of Radha and Krishna, or the *Geet Govind* of Jayadev. Similarly, shringar is the foundation on which the world of thumri stands, and is also the basis of the Bhakti and Sufi sentiments on which qawwalis and naatiya kalaam are composed. The other rasas besides shringar are more relevant to dance and drama, where dancers and actors must essay the emotions of anger (*raudra*), disgust (*vibhatsa*), compassion (*karuna*), heroism (*veer*), and wonderment (*adbhut*), among others.

A concept similar to the navarasa existed in ancient Greek mythology in the form of the Muses. They were believed to be goddesses, also nine in number, who were the daughters of Zeus and Mnemosyne. Each muse presided over a separate aspect of art and was the source of inspiration for all human creative endeavours – the fine arts, poetry, music, drama, and so on.

Lord Yehudi Menuhin was of the opinion that 'Indians had had more time to meditate than any other nation, and that they had put it to good use.' According to him, Indians realized that 'most of life's experiences have their exact time and place and music is no exception'.[1]

THROUGH THE AGES

The embryo of our music is found in the early Vedic chants of the second millennium BCE, which were formalized in the Sama Veda and went wherever Vedic philosophy flourished. While these liturgical chants remained the domain of the priestly class, a simultaneous, parallel stream of music was to be found among the common people. The liturgical type of music developed as *Margi* sangeet, which one can define as music along a defined path or marg, and the other came to be known as *Deshi* sangeet, or music of country or *deshi* origin. Consequently, our classical ragas are described as being either of *margi* or *deshi* origin, signifying whether a particular musical composition was conceived by learned pundits or adopted from a commonly popular melody. This distinction, though technically accurate, is now antiquated and both streams form a single corpus.

The music of India evolved as a monolithic entity from about 1500 BCE, through the classical ages of Emperor Ashoka (269-232 BCE), the Guptas (320-540 CE), and Harsha (606-647 CE). Monolithic entity here refers to the absence of external influences. Whatever came from outside, such as the advent of the Scythians in the first century AD (Kanishka and the Shaka calendar that starts from 78 AD) etc, became one with the host civilization, which continued to develop as an integrated, monolithic whole till the tenth century. The second ruler of the Gupta dynasty, Samudra Gupta (335-375 CE), was an accomplished poet and musician and one of his coins shows him playing the veena. The plays of poet-dramatist Kalidas were written during the reign of Chandra Gupta II (376-415 CE) and were set to music for public performance. The best-known treatise on sexual love, the *Kamasutra* was also written during the Gupta period, and the erotic sculptures of Khajuraho (tenth-eleventh century AD) are contemporaneous with this first stage of Indian music that lasted up to about 1000 CE. The period of the Guptas and Harshas is known as the Golden Age. It was so called due to the cultural and civilizational refinements that characterized the period. This is also when our indigenous music reached its acme of aesthetic excellence, just prior to the advent of external influence in the form of the Muslim incursions.

From these facts, it is evident that Hindustani classical music evolved in the geographical area associated with the historical eras mentioned above. This area extended from present-day Afghanistan (ancient Gandhara) in the west of the Indian subcontinent, to Bihar (ancient Magadh) in the east. What is present-day Bengal became part of it at a much later stage. Being essentially a tribal region at that time, the music of the north did not become popular till the late Sultanate and early Mughal periods, from the mid-fourteenth to mid-sixteenth centuries. Bengal would, however, go on to assume a position of preeminence in the development of Hindustani classical music during the nineteenth and twentieth centuries.

India had been absorbing foreign influences from the time of the Aryan influx of the second millennium BCE. This was followed by Alexander and the Greeks in the fourth century BCE, the Scythians (Kanishka) in the first century CE, and the Huns in the fifth century, all of whom would have contributed in some measure, no doubt, to Indian culture and civilization. After 1000 CE, India became the recipient of a new set of influences that would have a far greater impact on its culture than had ever been felt before. These new influences came by way of the incursions of the newly formed Muslim kingdoms and emerging Islamic cultures of Arabia, Persia, and Central Asia.

The newcomers brought with them their own music, primarily from Persia and Central Asia. A young Iranian musician, Sasan Bazgir, performed in Pune in March 2012, where he not only played the 'setar' an instrument quite akin to our sitar, but also discussed the similarities in the two traditions with the highly knowledgeable audience that Pune is renowned for. This influx of foreign traditions after the tenth century impacted our indigenous ethos and resulted in a blending of various musical traditions over the next five hundred or so years. A rich synthesis thus came about between the resident Vedic-Shastric stream on the one hand, and the incoming foreign streams on the other. The fusion of Bhakti, the Hindu concept of devotion, and Sufi, the Islamic concept of oneness with God, finally evolved into a composite whole that came to be called Hindustani shastriya sangeet, or Hindustani classical music.

For a variety of reasons, historical as well as geographical, these foreign influences did not permeate into the south, where the music continued almost in its original, *shastric* form. Technically, the differences between Hindustani and Carnatic streams are marginal, with many ragas being common to the two, though with different names. It is the musical styles and particularly their percussion instruments and rhythms that set the two apart. As a result of its cross-cultural cosmopolitanism, the northern school developed certain qualities of allurement and ornamentation which imparted a new and more refined sophistication to it. G.S. Balasubramanyam, eminent critic, commentator and Carnatic vocalist confirms this belief saying, 'Our (Carnatic) music has essentially remained the same through the centuries of tradition whereas the Hindustani system is more elastic and flexible and comparatively free from inhibitions and restrictions.'

Around 1237 CE, Saarang Dev, an eminent musicologist and sangeet shastri wrote his authoritative treatise, *Sangeet Ratnakar*, which provides a vital link between the earlier singular, insular *shastric* tradition, and the plural and cosmopolitan traditions that developed later. The latter tradition contains the contributions of three musical geniuses of medieval India – poet-musician Amir Khusrau of Delhi

(1253-1325), Naik Baijnath or Baiju Bawra (1486-1526), a singer in the royal court of Gwalior, and the saint-composer of Vrindavan, Swami Haridas (1480-1575).

The Mughal Empire occupies over 275 years of Indian history, from Babur's victory over the Lodhi sultans at Panipat in 1526, to the surrender of his sovereignty by the last emperor, Shah Alam II to the East India Company in 1803, after which the Mughals remained titular rulers till 1858. The synthesis that began in the tenth and eleventh centuries continued to flourish, and peaked in the mid-1500s. In my estimation, this acme of artistic excellence was reached in the person of Tanna Mishra, better known as Miyan Tansen (1506-1589), the court singer of Emperor Akbar at Agra. Some historians date Tansen from 1493 to 1586.

PROGRESSION OF INSTRUMENTAL MUSIC

Right from its birth as Vedic hymns to the time of Tansen 2,500 years later, the predominant mode of producing music was the human voice. The only musical instruments of note were the veena, associated with Saraswati, the goddess of learning and the flute (bansuri), associated with the divine cowherd, Krishna. The veena is undoubtedly of classical antiquity and had been around since ancient times. Among the various types of veenas, the Rudra veena is considered to be the oldest. The flute, however, remained restricted to its pastoral milieu and did not enter the classical sphere at all, till modern times. The modern-day sitar, the present-day sarangi (which evolved from the ancient *ravanhathha*), the sarod as it exists today, the santoor, and the violin, all joined the Indian classical music system only in the eighteenth century and later.

Whatever there was of instrumental music before the eighteenth century was largely restricted to playing second fiddle to the vocalist, though some contemporary instrumentalists persist in imparting a contrived and fanciful antiquity to their respective musical devices, despite empirical evidence to the contrary. The period of 200 years, from the mid-eighteenth to the mid-twentieth centuries, witnessed as many upheavals and transitions in music as it did in the history of the country. *Dhrupad*, the musical style of which Tansen was undisputed king in the mid-sixteenth century, would also undergo a major transformation in the dying days of the empire two centuries later with the emergence of khayal gayaki. In the eighteenth and nineteenth centuries, many new styles and musical instruments would make their entry on the stage.

Two other instruments existed in ancient India and were used for accompaniment only, in that they were vital to the music but were not 'stand alones' by themselves. The first of these is the four-stringed drone, the tanpura or tamboora, named after the Vedic sage, Tambooru Rishi. It is unique for the deep and rich resonance it produces, and is invaluable as the backdrop it provides for the performer. The second is the percussion instrument that would provide the rhythmic cycle for music. This was the pakhawaj, a two-sided drum played with both hands, which was the main percussion instrument till the eighteenth century. After that, the tabla gained prominence over the pakhawaj. The creation of the sitar is attributed to Amir Khusrau, who developed it primarily to obtain a simpler and readily portable version of the stately but ponderous veena. However, it was many centuries later that the sitar evolved into the modern, technically advanced musical device that we see today.

DHRUPAD: THE BEDROCK OF HINDUSTANI MUSIC

From the halcyon days of the Guptas in the sixth century, to the brilliance of Akbar's court in the sixteenth, Hindustani classical music enjoyed a place of reverence in society. Its development was governed by rules laid down by the great shastris of yore, and its reins remained in the hands of powerful guardians who regulated its performances at royal courts and according to specific norms.

Tansen had perfected the art of dhrupad singing, which was a style that had evolved over the past centuries and occupied centre stage in his day. The term comes from the combination of *dhruv* (constant) and *pad* (lyrics or style). It is a majestic mode of singing, demanding the highest artistic excellence, a robust physical constitution, and years of rigorous training. Its rhythm accompaniment is provided by the pakhawaj, which demands the same artistic excellence and physical vigour from its player, the pakhawaji, as does dhrupad from its singer, or the dhrupadiya.

Dhrupad gayaki (singing) is a grand, austere affair that requires a voice of extensive range, and is performed within a rigid, formal framework, as the term dhruv in its name signifies. Dhrupad singers believe that their music is ancient and originated from the seed syllable – *Aum*. Indeed, dhrupad involves breathing and sound patterns that are almost like a yogic discipline. A dhrupad recital evokes an ambience of profound spirituality, while allowing the performer to display his artistic virtuosity. The artistry of the latter at no point infringes on the sobriety of the former, maintaining a perfect balance between the two.

Dhrupad remained the principal singing style in Hindustani classical music up to the eighteenth century. Historically,

Raja Man Singh Tomar of Gwalior, who was Baiju Bawra's patron, is credited with developing and imparting the final polish to dhrupad gayaki around 1470 CE. Swami Haridas, Baiju Bawra and Tansen were more or less contemporaneous, with the Swami being the seniormost. All stayed at Raja Man Singh's court at some stage or the other. Though dhrupad had existed since the tenth century, it was really during Man Singh's reign that it achieved the final brilliance with which Tansen dazzled Akbar's court at Agra. Some scholars believe it to be the original Hindu style, devoid of Muslim influences. This is debatable since dhrupad steadfastly continued as the principal musical mode throughout the reign of the Mughals. As a forerunner of later and present-day styles, its significance remains undiminished. However, since the early twentieth century (and certainly since the advent of recording technology), khayal has become the predominant style. No doubt, members of the Dagar gharana, the Gundecha brothers, and others continue to sing dhrupad even now. Khayal retains many of the salient features of the dhrupad, particularly in the alap. Even now, many eminent dhrapudiyas continue to practise their art and teach this ancient style of singing to their younger generations.

4

The Age of Transition in Hindustani Classical Music

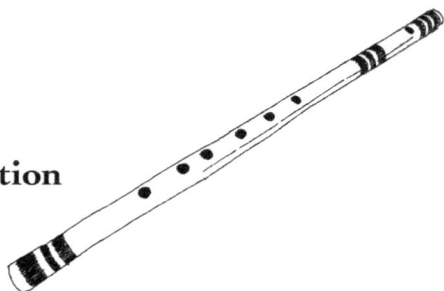

Aurangzeb, the last of the six great Mughals, died in 1707, and the empire went into steady decline thereafter. It reached its nadir with the invasion of the Persian adventurer, Nadir Shah, and his sacking of Delhi in 1739, during the reign of Muhammad Shah (1719-1748). Although he lost the Peacock Throne of his forebears to the marauder, it was during the reign of this same Muhammad Shah that the next, salient age in the evolution of Hindustani classical music dawned.

Muhammad Shah was given the appellation *Rangeela* (the colourful one) owing to his patronage of music and dance, and his life of fun and frolic. His empire was in dire straits, having broken up into petty regional satrapies ruled by his erstwhile vassals. Moreover, three powerful entities were rearing their heads to challenge the central power, in the persons of the Marathas, the Sikhs, and the Rajputs. Three foreign powers – the English, the French, and the Portuguese – had also come ashore to partake of their share of the cake that was India.

A NEW SPRING

Under these circumstances it was scarcely possible for music and the arts to remain unaffected. With the weakening of Mughal authority, regional satraps began to patronize their own favourites, and all the while, newer cultural influences continued to flow into India from the newly opened sea routes as well as the frequently traversed northwestern mountain passes.

This is also when new musical instruments began appearing in the numerous principalities and princedoms, some locally developed from older versions, and others that had been imported, improved upon, and adapted to existing styles. As a result of suffering repeated defeats at the hands of Nadir Shah in 1739, and Ahmed Shah Abdali (also called Durrani) in 1757-8, the Mughal nobility had become morally emaciated. It hardly had the stomach for the regulated formalities of the old courtly life. Dancing, hitherto restricted to Hindu temples and the Mughal court, also entered the cultural life of common people and began to flourish.

The sarod entered the Hindustani music sphere at this juncture, when some traders from Afghanistan, including those of the Bangash clan who dealt in horses, brought it to India. Its original form was the *rabab*, which continues to be so called and exists as a separate instrument in Iran, Afghanistan, and Kashmir. The term sarod, or *surode*, in the original Persian, simply means melody or song, as is evident from the Farsi phrase, *raqs-o-surode*, which literally means dance and music. The *rabab* has a wooden fret board, whereas its much improved variant, the sarod has one of metal, giving it a sharper, louder and more metallic sound. Ustad Hafiz Ali Khan (1888-1972), the great *sarodiya* and his equally illustrious son, Ustad Amjad Ali Khan, belong to the Bangash lineage whose ancestors came from Afghanistan and settled, first in Rewa and later in Gwalior, under the patronage of the Scindia rulers of that state.

The santoor, of Persian and Kashmiri folk origin, though extant in those days, did not enter the classical sphere till the mid-twentieth century. The chief architect of its appearance in a much improved and classically conducive form is Pandit Shiv Kumar Sharma, who came to be followed by several gifted performers such as Pandits Tarun Bhattacharya and Bhajan Sopori.

The Khayal

Hindustani music was now witnessing the birth of a new style to compete with the dhrupad. With the declining rigidity of court life, a relative informality had crept in, yielding space to a younger, more resilient musical mode. With Aurangzeb's death, the nobility as well as the citizenry won emancipation from the oppressive bigotry that his puritanical, forty-nine-year reign had imposed on public life. As a result, several of the arts and crafts of India experienced a vigorous resurgence. These developments were to have a major effect on music, which has lasted till the present day. The new musical mode that was evolving in the mid-eighteenth century came to be called khayal.

The term literally means imagination, thought, or idea. It liberated Hindustani music from its aesthetic straitjacket, and eased the demanding rigidity of dhrupad, allowing for greater artistic freedom both for the performer as well as the listener. There was a decline in emphasis on the austere rules that governed dhrupad, and an increased liberty to indulge in individual imagination, as the word khayal connotes. There was also a greater licence to entertain, though this license did not allow licentiousness. Neither classical purity nor musical merit was allowed to suffer during the evolution of the new style.

The transition from dhrupad to khayal was neither sudden nor complete. Indeed, both styles continued to exist side by side over the next two centuries. Even today, there are practitioners of great expertise of the old dhrupad gayaki, which is now witnessing a renaissance of its own. There is no doubt, however, that by the mid-twentieth century, khayal had achieved a definitive preeminence over its ancestor in the sensibilities of music lovers. Indeed, if we can call the fusion of indigenous and incoming Islamic streams in the tenth and eleventh centuries as the first re-flowering of music in India, the developments post-eighteenth century constitute its second phase.

Khayal, the new style of musical performance received wide and rapid appreciation, thus ensuring that the Indian musical tradition, far from going into decline with the Mughals, actually achieved even greater heights of artistic excellence. The most attractive feature in the evolution of khayal is the infusion of the element of surprise. This element of surprise, or spontaneity, is called *upaj*, literally, 'to sprout', which was lacking in dhrupad, where the form and sequence were constant. *Upaj* also refers to, among other things, an original idea or variation to a melody. As far as the classical aspect of Hindustani music is concerned, khayal occupies centre stage today.

Among the earliest exponents of khayal gayaki were a singer-composer duo, probably cousins, who are credited with being co-founders of this new form of music. Firoz Khan (*nom de plume*, Adarang) and Niyamat Khan (Sadarang) were singers in the court of Muhammad Shah 'Rangeela', and their twin mausoleums still stand today near the Qutab Minar at Mehrauli in Delhi. In fact, many of their famous khayal compositions are dedicated to their royal patron, whose name is mentioned in the lyrics even when they are sung today. Some musicologists attribute an even earlier evolution of the khayal to Amir Khusrau, which is not fully supported by empirical evidence. Khayal came into full flower much after Khusrau's time. Even if they were not its progenitors, Adarang-Sadarang can certainly be credited with giving final shape to khayal gayaki, as also with imparting to it the character of its present incarnation, irrespective of the earlier contributions of others.

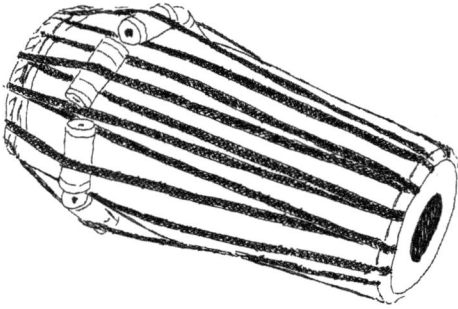

5

Predominance of
the Human Voice

One of the reasons why we hear so little about instrumental music in the annals of history is because it did not exist as an independent mode of musical expression till the cusp of the nineteenth-twentieth century. Through the millennia, vocal music remained the bedrock of the classical music traditions of India, Hindustani as well as Carnatic. The very edifice of Indian music rests on the human voice. Nothing comes even close to it in terms of modulation, flexibility, inflection and tonal purity. No musical instrument can match it for pitch, volume and timbre. Indians have always believed that the voice is the naturally perfect way of producing music. It is therefore incorrect to refer to vocal and instrumental music as two separate 'classifications' of Hindustani classical music. Such a classification is valid for archival reasons alone. Indeed, the standard bearers of our classical music over the last hundred years belong to both musical modes, vocal as well as instrumental.

Paradoxical as it may seem, in terms of the position stated above, instrumental music today has achieved a status at par with vocal music. If one were to take into account attendance at concerts and record sales, the former has in some cases surpassed the latter in popularity. I do not see a paradox here. The ease of assimilation and the soothing aftertaste of instrumental music accounts for its widespread appeal.

Before the advent of recording technology in the early twentieth century, musical performances were held in the palaces and mansions of the aristocracy, and audiences consisted largely of the elite. With recorded music becoming widely available, a huge segment of society was added to the listening public, not all of whom were familiar with the intricacies of classical music. New listeners found the instrumental version easier on the ear than the vocal, the effect of which can sometimes be disconcerting for beginners.

Each voice is peculiar to the human being it belongs to. The voices of two superlative singers may be as different as chalk and cheese. Listeners, especially novices, might find a particular vocalist's voice too gravelly, or his or her modulations too tempestuous, even unnerving. This is not the case with musical instruments. The sound of two sitars is near identical, differing only in the style of playing of the sitarist. The audio-visual effects of instrumental music, as compared to vocal, are also comparatively smooth and consistent. The atmosphere on stage at instrumental recitals in general and the demeanour of the performers in particular, is relatively calm, cool, and collected. Vocalists, on the other hand, are tempestuous in their mannerisms and often indulge in gesticulating and waving their arms about, which can throw novice listeners off balance. Beginners are, therefore, advised to embark on their musical journey by first listening to instrumental music and subsequently graduating to vocal, when they feel ready to do so.

Their journey of discovery must be a pleasurable one, and not an unpleasant chore. Even when they do begin to listen to vocal music, to start with they might want to pick lighter, semi-classical musical styles. A selection of music, listed progressively in order to make this transition from instrumental to vocal easy and seamless, is given separately. Nevertheless, newcomers to Hindustani classical music must be guided by the advice of two noted musicologists, Dr Narayan Menon, and O. Goswami:

- 'The grammar of music is absolutely essential for *right* singing. The sweet sounding-ness is not. A (sweet) voice is no more an asset to a vocalist than good handwriting is to a poet.'
- 'The human voice can range (far) wider over the whole gamut of human emotions (*ras-bhava*) than all the instruments.'[2]
- 'The voice is an instrument, not a conveyance for the lyrics of some composer. Words are simply the vehicle of tonal expression and therefore should be used at a minimum. It is the *swar* (note) carried on the vocal strings which evoke the aesthetic appeal of the raga, not the words. *Swar* is pre-eminent. Hence, the use of the human voice as an instrument.'[3]

Regarding the 'sweetness' of voice being immaterial to the merit of a recital, it is appropriate to cite an example, even an extreme one, to drive home the point. Gangubai Hangal, the great female vocalist of Kirana gharana (1913-2009), suffered a traumatic medical condition in mid-life, as a result of which her voice became heavy and deep, almost like a man's. Disregarding this misfortune, she continued to sing and turned her changed voice to her advantage, retaining her popularity among *rasiks* till the very end.

A novice who intends to become an informed listener must understand that vocal music is the root of the tree, and all other manifestations of music are its branches. It is imperative that a true *rasik* be able to appreciate good vocal music, however rough it may sound to his uninitiated sensibilities in the beginning. With time, he will begin to see through the rough edges and perceive the diamond within.

'Singing Style' in Instrumental Music

Besides the twelve-note scale of seven pure and five sharp and flat notes, Indian music recognizes ten additional microtones, taking the total number to twenty-two. These microtones are collectively called *shruti*; 'that which can be made audible'. The seven pure notes are fixed at shruti-s four, seven, nine, thirteen, seventeen, nineteen, and twenty-one.

Only those musical instruments which can produce the shruti can be included in Indian classical music. In this respect, the sarangi comes closest to the human voice's ability to produce the shruti. Since keyboard instruments cannot produce the shrutis, the harmonium is not a solo instrument in Hindustani classical music and is permitted only for accompaniment. It, therefore, follows that all music produced by means other than the voice – the branches, which are the instruments – must possess as many characteristics of the root, that is the voice, as possible. An instrument must produce music as the human voice would sing it. If it does not, it is not classical music.

Instrumental music cannot seek to replace the human voice, and instrumentalists are the first to acknowledge this fact. Thus instrumentalists must endeavour to play music as a singer would sing it, with the appropriate inflections and nuances. The closer an instrumentalist comes to the singing style, the better virtuoso he is. In fact, the eminent sarodiya, Ustad Amjad Ali Khan, says that when he is playing, he is actually singing to himself on the sarod (interviewed by Shekhar Gupta on the television programme, *Walk the Talk*, NDTV 24x7, 24 June 2007). This is called gayaki ang or the 'singing style' of instrument playing. It includes all the ornamental and decorative techniques that a vocalist might employ to embellish his singing. In this respect the great singer, Ustad Bade Ghulam Ali Khan and Ustad Vilayat Khan, the legendary sitarist were brilliant mirror images of each other in the vocal and instrumental streams respectively.

An important aspect of gayaki ang is the 'slide' technique of going from one note to another, which might be many notes away, without intermediate stops, in a single, unbroken, flowing motion. In vocal music, this technique is called *meend*, an arch-like movement that links the starting note to the destined one. In instrumental music, it is called *ghaseet*, literally, 'to slide'. For technical reasons, different instruments have a greater or lesser ability to achieve the tonal flexibility of a human voice. For instance, the ability to execute a ghaseet is restricted in the santoor, where its thirty-six pairs of strings are tuned to different notes and have to be struck with a curved, wooden mallet each time to produce sound. As such, it is impossible to 'slide' from one note, or string, to another. The santoor player, however, strikes the strings at great speed as he jumps from one to another in rapid succession, as to produce a sound exactly like a slide. In other instruments, such as the sarod, the ghaseet can be achieved with graceful ease. The meend is quite similar to the glissando in Western music.

As a rule, wind instruments like the shehnai and the flute, and bowed instruments like the sarangi and the violin, have a natural advantage in terms of their likeness to the human voice. This is because they can produce sustained, unbroken sound like the vocal chords. This is somewhat restricted in the sitar, where the player has to pluck the string repeatedly to sustain the sound. Even so, the sitarist is able to produce a marvellous and bewildering array of musical phrases by pulling the plucked string laterally and achieving remarkable, voice-like modulations. Other ornamental techniques like *harkat* and *gamak*, or grace notes, are embellishments of the main note and are achieved by lightly touching on its upper or lower neighbours.

A new trend was infused in the 1970s by the talented and innovative sitarist, Ustad Abdul Halim Jaafar Khan, of 'chromatic' notes. These are two notes played together, as in Western string instruments like the guitar. Shades of chromatic notes are also discernible in the sarod playing of Ustad Ali Akbar Khan. The great sitar virtuoso, Ustad Vilayat Khan (1928-2004), is considered the greatest exponent of the singing style of instrument playing in the entire canon of recorded Hindustani classical music. Such was his artistry in the gayaki ang of playing the sitar, that many vocalists became his shagirds (disciples). His recordings are widely available in India and abroad. These ornamental and decorative techniques are collectively called alankar. Alankar is fundamental to Hindustani music; integral, and not accidental, to it.

Two sitarists in their prime today – Pandit Budhaditya Mukherjee and Ustad Shahid Parvez – also have remarkable mastery over the gayaki style. The outstanding flautist, Pandit Hari Prasad Chaurasia, is of course a master of it. Although an instrumental performance is not called khayal in the absence of lyrics, in essence, it is the same thing and its movements and stages are identical to a vocal recital. Formally referred to as a rachna, 'creation' or an artistic or literary work, pieces of instrumental play might also be called the 'khayal style of playing'. The gayaki ang has been further facilitated by technical innovations in various plucked, bowed, and wind instruments over the last hundred years, allowing for a greater range and tonal flexibility.

Ustad Vilayat Khan's sitarist son, Shaujaat Khan has blossomed into a consummate artiste of the gayaki ang and is playing to packed houses in India, Europe and the US.

6

The Age of Gharanas

It is ironical that an event that was expected to sound the death knell of Hindustani classical music actually became the facilitator of its third and most magnificent renaissance. The British East India Company defeated the Nawab of Bengal in the Battle of Plassey in 1757. The next hundred years witnessed an uneasy truce between the dying Mughal Empire and the rising power of the Company, the latter increasingly laying claim to the rest of India. The Company had made Calcutta their capital, and Mughal Delhi began steadily losing its centrality as the political and cultural hub of India. Newer hubs came into being towards which musicians, composers, dancers, and artisans began to gravitate. Smaller in size and influence, and isolated from the old power centre, these new hubs were the durbars (courts) of the many princely states that had emerged after the demise of Mughal supremacy, and enjoyed a limited autonomy under the *Company Bahadur*, as the company was reverentially called.

This era heralded a renewed flowering of Hindustani classical music, its third, in even brighter colours than the first two. It occurred with the birth of the gharana tradition, a system that would nurture and sustain Hindustani classical music through its Golden Age, from about 1760 (after Plassey) to 1960 (the reorganization of the Republic of India into its present states). Midway through this period, the uprising of 1857 erupted, which the Company managed to suppress. The Mughal emperor was dethroned and exiled to Burma and in 1858, British paramountcy passed from the Company to the Crown.

During this golden age of Hindustani classical music, as the people of India lost political and economic power, and probably because of it, their latent genius began to manifest itself in what little was left in their domain – the sphere of the arts and culture. This is the age when India's arts and crafts, visual or performing, rural or urban, regional or cosmopolitan, folk or classical, achieved a crystallization that has lasted well into the twenty-first century. This is when the 'schools of painting' and fine arts, such as Kishengarh, Bundi, and Kangra, though extant from earlier times, came into their own. This is when the 'Bengal Renaissance' took place, producing intellectual giants like Bankim Chandra Chatterjee, the Tagores, and the Kalighat School of Art exemplified by Jamini Roy and Nandalal Bose.

The same applies to the schools of dance, particularly kathak, closely associated with Hindustani classical music, wherein the distinctive styles of Lucknow, Awadh, Jaipur, and Banaras evolved. Finally, this decentralization reached the schools of classical music. Where there had been one patron in the person of the Mughal emperor, now there were many. Many flowers had the opportunity to bloom, each redolent with its own fragrance. Many geniuses came to the fore in this golden age, and each one left his stamp on the arts, including music. These regional schools of music came to be called gharanas, literally families of musicians, who usually founded them under the patronage of their regional prince.

COLONIAL NEGLECT OF INDIAN MUSIC

By and large, British colonialists considered our music semi-barbaric. Some scholars, like Sir William Jones (1746-94), founder of the Royal Asiatic Society of Bengal in 1784, did make honest attempts to understand it, but their interest was largely antiquarian. A few musicologists like A.H. Fox-Strangeways also wrote a fair amount on the music of India. Books by both these gentlemen – *Music and Modes of the Hindus* by the former and *The Music of Hindoostan* by the latter – stand testimony to their genuine endeavours. Generally, however, the Colonialists as well as the Imperialists ignored the music of India, as they went about the task of establishing centres of higher learning in the three Presidencies of Madras, Calcutta, and Bombay.

While these centres received generous official patronage for the humanities and the sciences, classical music received none. In this context, it will be in order to quote from a leading British historian, Percival Spear, a keenly sensitive chronicler of India's ancient civilization.

In his book, *The Nabobs: Social Life in Eighteenth Century India*, he lucidly describes how callous and ignorant the early European settlers were towards the culture of India. 'The European, in general, was not aware of the riches of Sanskrit literature until, broadly speaking, the later years of the 18th century... the days of Warren Hastings and Sir William Jones... No European seems to have been able to appreciate Indian music.' The general verdict was summed up by Major J. Blakiston, 'In fact, they (Indians) have no music in their souls.'

The renowned German Indologist, Friedrich Max Müller, who undertook the first successful English translation of the *Rig Veda* in 1849, while he was a don at Oxford, also gave the music of India a miss. Despite these inglorious instances, it would be naïve, if not patently unfair, to tar the entire race with the same brush. Many Englishmen not only elicited a keen interest in Indian classical music, but also went to great lengths to extend a helping hand to its teaching along modern, scientific lines.

The callousness of the early years of British rule under the East India Company gave way to a more sympathetic attitude towards the culture of India after the transfer of power to the Crown in 1858. In fact, India owes much to the British imperialists, particularly after the end of the First World War in 1918 for their assistance in bringing about a renaissance in Indian classical music. There are many recorded instances of British scholars and musicians painstakingly organizing, analyzing, notating, and chronicling the essentials of Indian classical music, a practice that had been non-existent among the Indians themselves, who had left everything to memory and the guru-shishya parampara.

A New System

Soon, all the teaching of Indian classical music was taking place in the gharanas patronized by regional princes. Entertainment of their patrons being their primary aim, no research was conducted in the gharanas in the modern sense. The Gwalior gharana is considered to be the oldest, being the home of Tansen as well as of Baiju Bawra. Agra, and later Delhi, was the capital of the Mughal Empire. Both these also developed as gharanas, though the latter lost its distinction after the fragmentation of the Mughal Empire. Gharanas were usually named after their places of origin, such as Agra, Patiala, Rampur, Jaipur, and rarely like the Senia gharana, which was named after Tansen, though it was founded not by Tansen but by his sons, Taantarang Khan and Surat Sen, and disciples claiming ancestry to him.

Gharanas of instrumentalists, derived their names from the first prominent player who stamped it with his individual style. For example, Imdaad Khani Baaj was named after the grandfather of Ustad Vilayat Khan, and Jaafar Khani Baaj after the father of Ustad Abdul Halim Jaafar Khan. *Baaj* here refers to the distinctive style of playing of the founder. Practitioners of each gharana were direct descendents of its founder, followed by their extended families, and later, gifted pupils whom the reigning khaleefa (chief of the gharana) took under his wing. Each gharana is identified by its characteristic stylization of singing, playing, or dancing. For instance, Agra is known for its robust-voiced singing, Imdaad Khani Baaj for its refined gayaki ang of sitar playing, and Jaipur, by its scintillating footwork in kathak.

Some prominent gharanas of Hindustani classical music, along with their well-known proponents, are:

- Gwalior Gharana: Being the oldest, its modern founders at the court of the Scindias at Gwalior were Ustad Hassu Khan, Ustad Haddu Khan and Ustad Nathu Khan. Some prominent twentieth century Khayaliyas of the gharana are Pandit V.D. Paluskar, Pandit D.V. Paluskar, and Pandit Omkar Nath Thakur. Bringing in its second generation are Veena Sahasrabuddhe, Rajubhaiyya Poonchwale, Krishna Rao Pandit, and its present leading light, Ulhas Kashalkar. The Imdaad Khani Baaj of sitar playing is considered an offshoot of it, as are many other khayal gharanas also. This gharana is known for its skillful *taankari* and use of medium tempo even in slow khayals.

- Agra Gharana: Musicians of this gharana are supposedly descendants of Tansen from his daughter, Saraswati's side. Agra has the distinction of retaining the maximum characteristics of the old dhrupad gayaki, particularly in their nom-tom alap. Founded by Ustad Gagghe Khuda Baksh, its luminaries include *Aftaab-e-Mauseeqee* Ustad Faiyyaz Khan, Ustad Lataafat Hussain Khan, Ustad Vilayat Husain Khan and Lalith Rao. One of Faiyaaz Khan's disciples, Pandit Ratanjankar, pioneered the inclusion of Hindustani classical music as a permanent fixture on a nascent All India Radio. The Agra gharana is known for its robust, full throated singing and extensive *layakari*.

- Jaipur-Atrauli Gharana: It was founded by Ustad Alladiya Khan and its luminaries have been Pandit Mallikarjun Mansur, Kesarbai Kerkar, and Mogubai Kurdikar and the founder's two sons, Manji Khan and Bhurji Khan. Mogubai's daughter, Kishori Amonkar, was one of the most prominent Hindustani vocalists till recently but has cut down on appearances due to advancing age. Others in its contemporary roll of honour include Ashwini Bhide-Deshpande, Shruti Sadolikar, and Padma Talwalkar. Jaipur is noted for its highly intellectual raga *bandishes* and improvisational techniques and sustained *layakari*.

- Kiraana Gharana: Though named after a small town near Saharanpur in U.P., it developed mainly in the Dharwad region on the border of Maharashtra and Karnataka. This is the gharana that can be said to have been responsible for the resurgence of Hindustani classical music after its neglect during colonial rule. Founded by the legendary, honey-voiced Ustad Abdul Karim Khan, its shining stars have included Sawai Gandharv, Ustad Abdul Wahid Khan, Pandit Bhimsen

Joshi, Hirabai Barodekar, Basavaraj Rajguru, Prabha Atre, Jitendra Abhisheki, and Roshanara Begum.

- Patiala Gharana: It was jointly founded by Ustad Fateh Ali Khan and Ustad Ali Baksh, who were popularly known as 'Aliya-Fattu'. Its modern greats include the brothers, Ustad Bade Ghulam Ali Khan and Ustad Barkat Ali Khan, the former's son, Munawwar Ali Khan, and his son Raza Ali Khan, Naina Devi, and the ghazal-thumri doyenne, Begum Akhtar. Its present flag-bearers are Pandit Ajoy Chakraborty and his daughter, Kaushiki Desikan. Begum Parween Sultana is also part of this school, though she and her husband, Ustad Dilshad Khan, were also disciples of the sitar virtuoso, Ustad Vilayat Khan. It is renowned for its elaborate thumris and fast, shooting taans in khayal singing.

- Rampur-Seheswan Gharana: Founded by Ustad Inayat Khan, its trailblazers were Ustad Nissar Hussain Khan, and his illustrious shishya at Kolkata's ITC Sangeet Research Academy, Ustad Rashid Khan. Sulochana Brihaspati and Ustad Ghulam Mustafa Khan are among its other present-day luminaries.

- Maihar Gharana: Though not a gharana in the traditional sense, it was established by the eminent sarodiya of the Rampur gharana, Ustad Allauddin Khan. He went on to evolve his own style and established a music school at the erstwhile princely state of Maihar in central India. His first students were his son, Ali Akbar Khan, and daughter, Annapurna, a surbahar maestro, who married another shishya of the school, Ravi Shankar. Another sitar maestro, Pandit Nikhil Bannerji, who died prematurely, also trained here. The man who single-handedly pioneered the entry of the flute into the classical fold, Pandit Pannalal Ghosh, was also a student at Maihar. Many years later, the present doyen of the classical flute, Pandit Hari Prasad Chaurasia, famously parked himself at a reluctant Annapurna Devi's doorstep in Mumbai and refused to budge till she relented and accepted him as her disciple. She eventually did, and the results are there for the world to see.

- Dilli (Delhi) Gharana: It was established by Amir Khusrau himself in the fourteenth century during the reign of Allauddin Khilji, but its members got scattered after the sacking of Delhi by Nadir Shah in 1739. Its present khaleefa, Ustad Iqbal Ahmed Khan, claims that members of the gharana returned after the First War of Indian Independence in 1857, and resettled in the Daryagunj area but could not regain their earlier stature.[4] Some of its other well-known names are Ustad Chand Khan and Nissar Ahmed Khan. It remains closely associated with the organization of the annual Jahaan-e-Khusrau festival in the memory of its founder, initiated by film director-artist-designer and aesthete-at-large, Muzaffar Ali, who has also made the award-winning film, *Umrao Jaan*.

- Other Gharanas: Mewati, Bhendi Bazaar, and Banaras gharanas produced such luminaries as Pandit Jasraj (Mewat), Ustad Amir Khan (Bhendi Bazaar, also associated with the now-defunct Indore Gharana), Girija Devi, and Rajan and Sajan Mishra (Banaras). Lata Mangeshkar also claims allegiance to Bhendi Bazaar through her guru, Ustad Aman Ali Khan, son of the gharana founder, Ustad Chhajju Khan.

This golden age of gharanas lasted till about 1960, by when all the erstwhile principalities had been dissolved and the Indian Republic was reconstituted in the form in which it exists today. Thereafter, increased societal mobility and a freer mixing of the populace resulted in a dilution of the individuality of the gharanas. Those who were in their prime continued their individualistic gayaki even after 1960, as did their followers, for another decade or two, till the gharanas began merging into one another. Nevertheless, the pleasant after effects of gharanedar gayaki linger on, and many leading musicians still subscribe to the old styles and recall their gurus with pride and gratitude.

While the gharanas differed in style and nuance, the classical principles of antiquity were uniformly followed everywhere. Nevertheless, due to the absence of a central authority to monitor their growth, coupled with the idiosyncrasies of individual khaleefas and their patrons, there remained a real danger of the music losing its classical purity. Individual gharanas had been going their separate ways for over a century, and there was a chance that some would go astray. The authentic core of this ancient art thus faced a risk of dilution and decline, if not outright loss.

The need of the hour was to halt this trend by formalizing an ancient tradition that had been passed over many generations through the guru-shishya parampara, and to collate it into an organized and centrally monitored corpus. A modern, scientific framework of classification, codification and notation was required for this corpus, from which future generations could draw material for their artistic growth. This would also ensure that the artistic integrity of the musical heritage remained intact.

CHATUR PANDIT: THE SAVIOUR

This feat was successfully achieved by Pandit V.N. Bhatkhande (1860-1935), also known as 'Chatur Pandit' of Bombay (now

Mumbai). He carried out a historic survey of the entire music of India, and recapitulated its essentials into a working system based on sound, classical foundations. A creative genius, he took this first and vital step towards regeneration and revival at a significant time, thereby placing Hindustani music under his deep obligation. His magnum opus in six volumes, titled *Kramik Puʃtakmaalika*, was published after forty years of painstaking and tireless study. It forms the basis of all formal teaching of Hindustani classical music today. Had he not intervened, a magnificent heritage could well have been lost to the whims of its feudal patrons or the fancies of its semi-literate practitioners.

The very first All India Music Conference (and concert) was organized by Pandit Bhatkhande at Baroda in 1916, and was presided over by the ruling prince of the state, Maharaja Sayajirao Gaekwad III (1875-1939). A centre for teaching music, Marris College, was established in Lucknow, named after Sir William Marris, Governor of the United Provinces, who presided over the fourth All India Music Conference in 1925. Marris College was later selected to be the nucleus on which the Bhatkhande Music University stands today, and continues to contribute significantly to the scientific teaching of Hindustani classical music. Modern innovations in acoustics and recording techniques, as well as changing public taste have come into play, but the foundation laid and nurtured over the ages through the guru-shishya parampara, now formally collected, collated and codified, has survived the ravages of time.

Another great musicologist-musician, Pandit V.D. Paluskar (1872-1931) of Gwalior, also contributed much in this respect, particularly by restoring the social respectability of Hindustani classical music in Indian society at large, especially among upper-class Hindu families. Hindustani music had lost much of its early dignity by the end of the nineteenth century due to its condemnation by British imperialists as a form of depravity, indulged in only by the debauched and profligate Indian aristocracy. Consequently, it had come to be regarded as disreputable by the Indian elite, particularly the upper classes.

Paluskar valiantly liberated the intelligentsia from the puritanism of their Victorian overlords, as a result of which his own, as well as Bhatkhande's ethnic community, the Maharashtrians, became the first to take up the challenge of restoring this fallen art to its rightful place of pride in the culture of India.

GLOBAL APPEAL TODAY

Although Hindustani classical music has regained its place as a tradition of refinement and sophistication, the universality of its appeal has diminished with the growing popularity of other forms of music, particularly after the television and IT revolutions of the late twentieth century. Still, among the initiated, it continues to exert a magnetism that sustains its underlying charm. The gharanas might have largely disappeared, but their influence remains. The number of performers might have ebbed in the last quarter of the twentieth century, but there have been enough of those who stood their ground and succeeded in making their mark, and are now much sought after by recording studios and concert audiences alike, both at home and abroad. What has also undergone a decline is the number of informed listeners.

Even so, the twenty-first century is showing promising signs of a renewal among performers who are keen to present this ancient art to an increasingly globalized and modernized audience in a newer, and more commercially viable, format. There is also a palpable interest in Hindustani classical music globally. Not only are people coming to India to learn, but many Indian musicians, known and unknown, have set up schools in the West to teach music. For example, the great sarodiya, Ustad Ali Akbar Khan, who passed away in 2009, spent much of the last fifty years of his life in California. For a period in the 1990s, Pandit Hari Prasad Chaurasia would teach for four months a year as part of the faculty at the World Music Conservatory at Rotterdam. Sarangi maestro Pandit Ram Narain has done pioneering work with classicists in European conservatories, and tabla wizard Ustad Zakir Hussain spends his time equally at home and abroad.

Ravi Shankar, the greatest international guru of them all, while appreciative of the growing interest of the West in the music of India, has bitter memories of foreign attitudes in bygone days, as is obvious in what he writes in a foreword to the book, *The Music of India*, by Peggy Holroyde, 'It is ironic to see the interest in our music that exists in Great Britain these days, since in all the 200 years or more of association with India, the British never, never took any interest, and in fact they even looked down on it, thinking that our vocal music was like gargling, and such things *(sic)*. Even the sound irritated them, and the only people during those years who took a sympathetic view were a very few music scholars who wrote books trying to interpret Indian classical music for the people of the West.' Besides being his general observation about the British attitude, he also cites a personal example during an interview by the BBC (in two parts) on the occasion of his eighty-third birthday: he recalled how some

Western critics used to equate the sounds of the sitar (while improvizing in the upper octave during alap and jod) with the 'mewing of a kitten'.

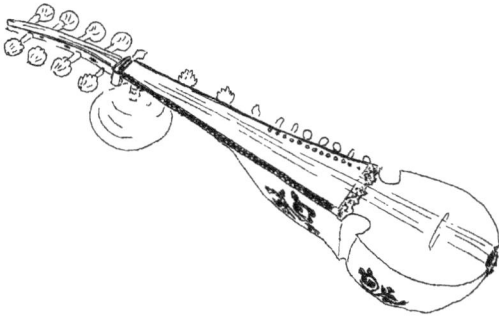

7

Raga Sangeet

What has been known as Hindustani classical music or Bharatiya shastriya sangeet all through the years, has now been given the new and inclusive, generic term **Raga Sangeet** by musicologists. This term encompasses all the old and new forms of singing and instrumental playing of raga-based music, including the old dhrupad gayaki, the currently pre-eminent khayal gayaki, as well as the lighter, semi-classical modes like thumri and dadra.

THE RAGA

To appreciate raga sangeet, we must understand the term 'raga' to begin with. It has been variously interpreted. At one end of the spectrum it is considered to be some sort of a mystical phenomenon associated with the supernatural, and on the other end, has been likened to American Jazz. Without getting into semantics, raga can be described in simple terms, as has been done in the Oxford English Dictionary (OED) 'a pattern of (musical) notes used as a basis for improvization'.

This succinct description carries within it the kernel of truth, from which we can derive the full meaning of raga. That truth lies in the phrase, 'basis for improvization'. All raga sangeet is improvization using a given pattern of notes.

Another definition of raga is given by the critically acclaimed musician, demonstrator and researcher, Pandit Amarnath (1924-97), often called 'a musician's musician', of the Indore gharana, who explains it as follows: 'Roughly translated, the phrase *ranjayatee itee ragaaha* (in Sanskrit) means "that which pleases (aesthetically) is raga." The raga forms the basis of Indian classical music; it is a scheme of five, six or seven notes composed logically, the layout of notes evolves into a significant form. Each raga has its own accent, each its rules.'

Other musicologists have explained it as follows: 'Raga is a series of five or six musical notes upon which a melody is founded. Each raga has its own specific features, elements and moods that define it.' (*Khayal*, a documentary film directed by Usha Deshpande in which Pandits Ravi Shankar and Shiv Kumar Sharma explain the concept of raga, gharana etc., screened at Nandan cinema hall, Kolkata on 17 April 2008).

RAS-BHAVA

In the light of the descriptions given above, it becomes apparent that certain aspects of raga cannot be explained in precise, scientifically coherent terms. For instance, how is this improvization to be executed? What are the principles that govern it? This is where the aural guild tradition, the guru-shishya parampara described earlier, comes in and which, as per some pandits, renders such precision beyond the pale of explanation. If, however, our aim is simply to understand the basis of raga sangeet in order to enjoy its aesthetic beauty, do we really need to plumb such depths that defy literary description and can only be imparted by a guru to a shishya?

What we have is a tune, a melody of five, six or seven musical notes. A tune is a tune, in raga sangeet just as it is in any other musical tradition. What is unique in a raga is its emphasis on mood-emotion, or ras-bhava. Hindustani classical music can be referred to as 'contemplative music'. There are two contemplators – the musician who is crafting his contemplation with his musical imagination, and the listener who is absorbing the contemplation aurally. For this encounter to be complete, their contemplations must unite. Other than this meeting occurring 'in the mind's eye', or in the imagination of the two contemplators, there is another, distinctly personal aspect to this encounter, which is also a time-honoured one in the Indian musical ethos.

This is the concept of a physical convergence through eye contact between the musician and the listener, and is called in Hindustani, *aankhen chaar karna*, 'the coming together of four eyes', two each of the co-contemplators. This concept characterizes the chemistry between the musician and the lover of music. This chemistry holds good even in a concert hall, where a single performer is regaling an entire audience. This concept is not peculiar to raga sangeet but exists at the heart of all types of music, including worship.

Religious pilgrimages have been undertaken in India since time immemorial. The object of a pilgrimage is to pay obeisance to a deity at a temple dedicated to it. This obeisance is called darshan and literally means the pilgrim obtaining a glimpse of the deity and, in turn, being blessed by the latter's benevolent gaze falling upon him. A darshan is complete only when the devotee comes physically before the idol of the deity and gazes at it, and vice versa. The same holds true for pilgrimages to Sikh gurdwaras and Muslim mausoleums, neither of which house any idols. It is worth mentioning that in gurdwaras, superlative Hindustani music is sung in the form of shabad keertan and *aasa ∂i vaar*. Similarly, the best qawwaali can be heard at dargahs like the ones dedicated to Sheikh Nizamuddin Auliya in Delhi and Khwaja Moinuddin Chisti in Ajmer.

Raga sangeet is also called mood music due to its singular emphasis on emotion. Like its many other aspects, this too may not be easy to describe in words. But its essence will surely be discernible to the sensitive mind. When one listens to a raga, its pattern of musical notes arouses a distinct emotion in the brain. The combination of the notes of the raga and the emotions they arouse is known as its ras-bhava. This ras-bhava will automatically and invariably be perceived whenever one listens to that particular raga, whatever its mode of rendition, vocal or instrumental.

Different ragas invoke different mood-emotions. This is also referred to as the power of music to transform and transport the mind to another place. For instance, Raga Pahari, which literally means 'of the hills', never fails to transport the mind to the beautiful hills and valleys of the Himalayas. This implies that the ras-bhava of a raga lies in its 'pattern of musical notes' as the OED describes it, and Pandit Amarnath explains it. It is here that the oft-mistaken references to the mystical and the supernatural come into play.

How are these mood-emotions aroused? The ras-bhava that we experience lies in the genius of the composer who set the musical notes of a raga in that specific pattern, possibly centuries ago. The art of evoking the mood-emotion of each raga is taught to the musician by his guru, by a method carried over the millennia through the aural guild tradition. Each raga has its distinct ras-bhava, a mood lent to it by the emotion it engenders. This mood is experienced by both the contemplators – the musician while rendering it, and the *rasik* while hearing it. Ras-bhava is intrinsic to raga sangeet and teaching the pupil how to evoke it lies at the core of the guru-shishya parampara.

Another aspect of historical detail that merits attention is the association of particular ragas with segments of the twenty-four-hour cycle of the day. This cycle has been divided into eight segments of three hours each, called a pehar or shift. These shifts are – early morning, late morning, afternoon, evening, night, late night, midnight and dawn. For instance, Raga Lalit, literally, 'beautiful', is a popular early morning raga, well-loved by musicians and listeners alike. On hearing it, the listener will invariably experience an emotion of tranquility and calm associated with a beautiful dawn. The celebrated filmmaker, Bimal Roy, used it to telling effect in his 1955 masterpiece, *Devdas* (music by S.D. Burman). In the morning, as a girl fills her pitcher at the village pond, Lalit is played in the background on the sarod and, with a forward flash, the girl grows into a young woman.

Ras-bhava has also been described as the singer's technique of 'musical-acting' or 'vocal-acting'. Pandit Birju Maharaj (in the interview to Mrinal Pande, ibid) refers to this as 'tying knots in the air' (*hawa mein gaanth baandhanaa*). Ragas are also associated with the cycle of the seasons. These are *shishir* (winter), *basant* (spring), *greeshma* (summer), *megha* (monsoon), and *hemant/sharad* (autumn). They have also been likened to the sounds of birds, such as the Carnatic Raga Hansadhwani, which means 'sound of a swan'.

The association of music with the cycle of time and seasons further enhances the colours of the mind engendered by the raga in accordance with its ruling ras, mood or muse, be it the love of a devotee for a deity, separation from or longing for the beloved, and so on. This is how ras-bhava is evoked, by association of a raga with its ruling sentiment, time of rendition, and seasonality. This comes out vividly whenever, however, and in whichever genre it is performed. As far as music is concerned, the ruling ras is *shringar*. Within it or from it, other rasas such as *bhakti, karuna,* or *shant* may ensue. The other rasas, particularly *hasya, raudra, veer,* and *adhbut* are more relevant to dance and drama.

THE PAKAD

Each raga has a distinctive *pakad*, which literally means to grip, which is its main musical phrase that distinguishes the raga, and invokes its primary emotion in the mind that gives the raga its ras-bhava. No two ragas will have the same *pakad*, even if they are made up of similar notes. Musical notes are set in such a pattern that the *pakad* of each raga will be unique to it and, to the informed ear, render it instantly recognizable. *Pakad* is that feature which distinguishes a raga from other, similar-sounding ragas, and which lends to it its distinctive mood-emotion. The *pakad* of a raga is its singular identity.

INDIAN JAZZ

So far, there seems nothing in raga sangeet that is not found in other great musical traditions as well. Mozart, Tchaikovsky and Beethoven have all evoked human emotions through music. This brings us to the second aspect of the raga as 'a pattern of musical notes, used as a basis for improvization', as described by the OED. This implies that while every recital of a Mozart composition will always be the same in content, irrespective of its performer, every recital of an Indian raga will invariably be different, even when performed by the same musician.

This is because Western classical music is formally structured in its entirety, where the length and volume of each note and the rhythm and tempo at each stage of the composition have been specified in writing. They have to be perfectly right each time the composition is played. Moreover, a symphony orchestra has a conductor to synchronize the playing of all the members of an ensemble in accordance with the sheet music provided. Raga sangeet, on the other hand, has no sheet music, and lays down the barest, though strictest, framework, thus leaving the performer to his own devices as long as he remains within that framework.

To return to Pandit Amarnath's definition of the raga, the individual ingenuity of the artiste comes from his interpretation of the pattern of notes and his improvizations thereon. This is why raga sangeet is often likened to jazz. Raga sangeet is like portrait painting. When a musician performs a particular raga, he paints a portrait of it. And each time he performs the same raga, he paints another original, and not a copy of the previous version. It is well known that improvization on a given melody or 'pattern of notes' is also the spirit of jazz. In this respect, the likeness of raga sangeet to jazz is evident. Jazz, by definition, is music as interpreted by various musicians playing the same composition. Except for the 'greats' like Ellington, Armstrong, Miles Davis, Dave Brubeck and their modern counterparts who compose their own music, most popular jazz, even when played by famous musicians, is in the form of interpretations of well known 'standards' by different artistes. A composition that has achieved wide popularity and iconic status or become associated with its composer is called a 'standard'. Examples of such standards are: *Take the 'A' Train* composed by Billy Strayhorn (the pianist in Duke

Ellington's band, it became the signature tune of Voice of America's long-running weekly programme, Jazz Hour); *Take Five* composed by Paul Desmond (saxophonist of the Dave Brubeck Quartet), and *Desafinado*, a brilliant bossa nova composition by Antonio Carlos Jobim, and made famous by American saxophonist Stan Getz and guitarist Charlie Byrd, besides a vocal rendition of it by superstar actor/singer, Dean Martin called *Slightly out of Tune*.

This is the remarkable similarity of jazz with Hindustani classical music, where the same ragas are variously interpreted and improvized upon by different musicians. Generally, jazz is enjoyed most when the listener is more or less familiar with the number being played, and is thus better able to appreciate a musician's interpretation of it. The same is also true of raga sangeet. The *rasik's* pleasure is greatly enhanced when he is able to identify the raga and thereby fully enjoy the performer's improvizations on it.

Apart from aiding in the identification of the raga, the *pakad* also plays another important role in the recital. The perceived mysticism of raga sangeet lies in its unique ability to repeatedly arouse those same mood-emotions in the listener's mind today, as its original composer intended centuries ago. It is the *pakad* that enables the arousal of this ras-bhava. The talented young singer, Ms Shruti Sadolikar has used an innovative phrase; 'liquid architecture' to describe this phenomenon that otherwise defies any description.

CLASSIFICATION OF RAGA SANGEET

Raga sangeet is often categorized as 'classical' and 'semi-classical'. Such a categorization is mainly for purposes of cataloging. No musician worth the name can survive in the field without being equally adept in both categories. It is true that an artiste may feel more at home and achieve greater success in one genre than in the other, but that is a matter of choice, his own as well as that of his listeners.

Generally, dhrupad and khayal are termed classical, and all others, semi-classical. All raga sangeet is raga-based. The same raga can be sung in any genre, classical or semi-classical, and played on any musical instrument. Thumri, one of the most popular forms of semi-classical music, can also be sung as accompaniment to kathak, or in the form of a ghazal, which is a form of Urdu poetry.

Raga sangeet is a ductile monolith that can be sculpted into myriad shapes. Each sculpture can stand alone, while remaining connected with the parent. Thus, classifications are not hidebound and exclusive. They neither diminish the achievements of a gifted musician who might specialize in a semi-classical mode, nor enhance those of a less-talented one who might perform in the classical genre.

A truly great practitioner of raga sangeet will acquit himself with equal aplomb in all its sub-genres. Such a practitioner is called a *chaumukhi gayak* (four-sided or multi-faceted singer/performer) who is equally competent in all spheres of music. Such practitioners were vocalists Ustads Bade Ghulam Ali Khan, Amir Khan and Pandit Bhim Sen Joshi; and instrumentalists Ustads Vilayat Khan (sitar), Ali Akbar Khan (sarod) and Pandit Pannalal Ghosh (flute) in the last century. Presently, vocalists like Pandit Ajoy Chakraborty, Ustad Rashid Khan, and Vidushi Kishori Amonkar, and instrumentalists Ustad Shahid Parvez (sitar), Pandits Hari Prasad Chaurasia (flute), and Shiv Kumar Sharma (santoor) are in their prime. Leading lights of the future are going to be vocalists Shruti Sadolikar, Ashwini Bhide Deshpande and Arshad Ali and instrumentalists Purbayan Chatterji (sitar), Rakesh Chaurasia (flute), and the brothers Ayaan and Amaan Ali (sarod).

8

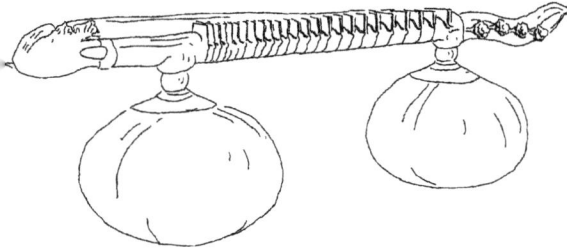

Ingredients of Raga Sangeet

Note, tempo and rhythm are the three ingredients that are vital to all music. In the Hindustani tradition, they are called *swar* (note), *laya* (tempo), and *taal* (rhythm). A fourth aspect, *bol* (lyrics), is not an ingredient and is used only to enhance the mood that a raga seeks to evoke by infusing a poetic facet to its vocal rendition. In fact, an excessive emphasis on lyrics contravenes the centrality of the musical core. Had this not been so, it would be hard to explain how accomplished instrumentalists manage to achieve the magical transcendence that they do.

This further reinforces the quintessence of the melodic pattern of notes that lies at the root of a raga. There are musicologists who go so far as to say that the human voice is itself an instrument. Words are merely tonal expressions to carry a melody, and should be restricted to a minimum. It is pertinent to quote from an interview on 16 June 2009 given in Kolkata by Javed Akhtar, one of the finest lyricists in India today, (reported in the *Telegraph*, Kolkata). 'Words should not describe feelings…just a few words cannot fathom the depths of any emotion. Words should only give a hint… should touch the tip of the iceberg. Let the iceberg be the imagination of the listener. If the listener is not contributing, it's bad art. One should always keep space for the sensitive ear. Only when there is a mutual process, can it be called art.'

This mutuality is reiterated by Ethel Rosenthal in her book, *The Story of Indian Music*, written in 1928. In it she says, 'In Indian music, the art of the listener equals the importance and skill of the interpreter (musician).' This is what sets raga sangeet apart from bhajans (hymns), where the lyrics stress religious symbolism and the music, however superlative, remains repetitive and mechanical. Hindustani classical music is not merely a joyous enterprise. It is much more, a spiritual one, a sadhana, as Pandit Ravi Shankar puts it. It carries within it an element of devotion. It is not merely the personal achievement of the performer producing music. He is creating something beautiful for humanity. His music itself is worship; hence, the near absence of bhajan-singing in Hindustani classical music.

As regards the role of the *rasik*, this is what Ustad Shahid Parvez, who along with Pandit Budhaditya Mukherjee is arguably the best sitarist around these days, has to say: 'The *rasik* needs to develop the art of listening to the same degree as does the performer' whom he is listening to. Every musician (*sangeetkaar*) must first become a listener or *sunkaar* (from *sun*, or to listen). A good *sunkaar* is one who is neither over critical (intent on fault finding) nor over emotional (developing a pro or con bias) but an equanimous co-contemplator with the performer. (Interviewed in *Sur Saptak*, a weekly programme on Lok Sabha TV, anchored by Bindu Chawla, daughter of Pandit Amarnath and a learned musicologist herself.)

The second vital ingredient of raga sangeet, is *laya*, the tempo at which a composition is rendered, which can be slow, medium, or fast. *Taal*, the third facet, is the rhythm cycle to which the composition is set. A raga can have compositions set to any *taal*, while every *taal* can be rendered in any *laya*.

BANDISH: A MUSICAL COMPOSITION

While *swar* (note) remains pre-eminent in the rendition of a raga, when it comes together with the other two components, *laya* (tempo) and *taal* (rhythm), it forms a *bandish*, which literally means a 'knotted up' composition of all three. The *bandish* contains within it that pattern of notes that the OED speaks of, and which will be the basis of the performer's improvizations, which lie at the heart of raga sangeet. For each raga, this pattern of notes is fixed and no notes other than these can be used while performing it. Also fixed is the sequence in which these notes are to be used, both in the ascending and descending scales. The ascent is called *aarohan* and the descent *avarohan*.

Within this pattern of notes and their sequence of use, there are many permutations and combinations using which a *bandish* can be created. Thus, any number of *bandishes* might be composed in a raga and they can be performed in the classical or semi-classical sub-genres. Also, they can be set to any taal cycle of the composer's choice. The artiste can decide which tempo he wishes to perform a *bandish* at. Unlike in a Western music recital, the Hindustani classical musician plays three roles simultaneously. He is the composer, conductor and performer.

Add to this the unique improvizational character of raga sangeet and we can understand why each recital of the same raga, in the same *bandish*, even by the same performer, is invariably different. However, the rules regarding the pattern of notes, their sequence of use and the *pakad* of the raga are inviolable. *Bandishes*, each with their poetic lyrics and set to different taal cycles, have been conceived by composers and passed on from teacher to pupil over the centuries. An odd raga here and there, which might have lost its defining character in transition and caused confusion as a result, might be scrutinized by musicians over the years and standardized, the seal of authority stamped on it by an eminent *khaleefa*, thus securing it for future generations.

In the past, raga controversies arose because of the lack of written records (notation) etc. There were ragas with the same notes and structure that had different names in different gharanas. Musically they bore no differences or had the most negligible differences. Thus the need for a common platform was felt, where representatives of different gharanas came together, standardized raga names, and gave coherence to the fast evolving grammar of raga sangeet. This feat was achieved to a great extent by Pandit V.N. Bhatkhande, among others, as mentioned earlier.

Notwithstanding such exceptions, a *bandish* will invariably retain the distinctive *pakad* and *ras-bhava* of the parent raga. This, in essence, is a result of the guru-shishya parampara. Every composition, whether in the classical, semi-classical, or light-classical genre, is called a *bandish*. A *bandish*, along with all its parts, constitutes a Hindustani classical music recital.

Parts of a Bandish

Bandishes, be they in any genre, classical, light or semi-classical, vocal or instrumental, comprise two main parts. The first or opening part defines the main composition and is usually in the middle octave. This is called the *sthaayi*, which in Sanskrit means static, lasting or permanent. The second part acts as a counter to the first, and touches the higher reaches of the scale. This is called the *antara*. The *sthaayi* contains the *pakad* of the raga, which gives it its identity. The *sthaayi* is always constant, whereas the *antara*, being intermediate, may be different, or there might be more than one *antara* in a *bandish*, though in most cases, there is only one. *Antara* is the root word for intermediate, meaning second or following, after the first, static *sthaayi*. In popular parlance, the *sthaayi* is also called *mukhda* or the face of the *bandish*. The *sthaayi* and *antara* together make up a complete *bandish* composition.

9

Concert and Recital

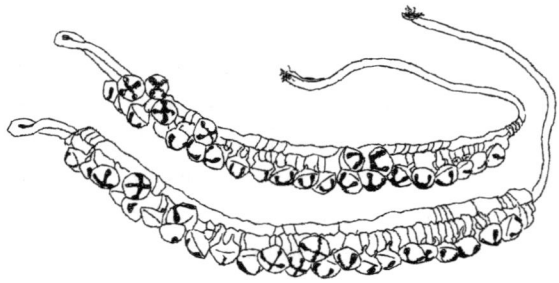

THE ATMOSPHERE AT CLASSICAL MUSIC RECITALS

From the first modern concert held at Baroda in 1916, to the present day, auditoria and their acoustics have changed a great deal. In feudal times, the court of a prince or the mansion of a zamindar was the usual venue for *baithaks* (sittings). The audience consisted of the local elite. The musicians and their audience sat on mattresses spread on the ground.

Modern concerts are open to the public. Concert venues now include alfresco auditoria in the old Greco-Roman style, which have become quite fashionable in metropolitan cities. Sound-proof theatres and high resolution microphones have changed the character of live performances. However, the atmosphere at Hindustani classical music concerts continues to be informal, reminiscent of the *baithaks* of old. There is no 'white tie' tradition, and men and women don their varied traditional attires, be it dhoti-kurta in the east, the kurta-pyjama in the north and west, or the heavy silks favoured by women in the south. Some gentlemen may come in suits and youngsters in jeans. All are acceptable. There is an air of bonhomie all around, which engulfs musicians and listeners alike.

In India, there is also a long-standing tradition of open and unabashed appreciation by the audience of a performer's artistry, even in the middle of a recital, whenever he executes an attractive or complex *tukda* with élan. Such appreciation usually bursts forth in the form of clearly audible *wah! wah!*, which can be disconcerting to those unprepared for this accepted practice.

THE EVOLUTION OF CONCERTS AND RECITALS

Till the 1960s, a music event was called a music conference or *sangeet sammelan*, a term corresponding to an assembly of musicians. Some of them became regular fixtures at certain venues, and began to be referred to as Utsav, or festival, such as the Shankar Lal Festival in Delhi and the Harvallabh Festival in Jalandhar. The Dover Lane Conference in Kolkata is among the oldest and most prestigious of such festivals. These festivals or conferences can last from a couple of days to a week. Each day's events are collectively termed a concert. Some festivals now also include dance, like the Khajuraho Utsav held at the famous temples of the same name, near Jhansi in Madhya Pradesh.

A concert may last from three to five hours, with some being all-night affairs. A recital includes a raga-based *bandish* in any of its forms – a classical khayal (vocal or instrumental), a semi-classical thumri or dadra, or the rarer dhrupad. A day's concert might feature single or multiple recitals, each presented by one or more artistes in any of the sub-genres mentioned. We will discuss only a khayal recital since it is the main item in a classical musician's repertoire. He may follow it up with a thumri or dadra, or rarely, even a bhajan sung in the raga-sangeet style.

A khayal recital, vocal or instrumental, may last from forty-five to ninety minutes. Generally, it has a musician performing alone, with three or four accompanists. The eminent instrumentalists Pandit Ravi Shankar and Ustad Ali Akbar Khan started a trend in the 1950s, where two principal musicians played together. This was termed *jugalbandi* (partnership). It became increasingly popular and has seen musicians combine the sarod and violin, the violin and shehnai, the flute and santoor, and so on. Examples of such jugalbandis are: sarod and violin (Ustad Ali Akbar Khan and Pandit V.G. Jog), violin and shehnai (V.G. Jog and Ustad Bismillah Khan) and flute and santoor (Pandits Hari Prasad Chaurasia and Shiv Kumar Sharma).

This practice of jugalbandi had been in vogue among some gharanas of vocalists even earlier, where two main singers would perform together. In fact, in the Sham Chaurasi gharana of Hoshiarpur, Punjab, duets were a tradition. The last popular duo of this gharana – Ustad Nazaakat Ali and Ustad Salaamat Ali Khan – was known for their melodious voices and their highly stylized improvisatory technique. The Singh Bandhu is another duo famous for its vocal jugalbandi, as are the brothers, Rajan and Sajan Mishra of the Banaras gharana. Jugalbandi is not to be confused with vocal support provided by a second singer, which often happens during concerts where the principal singer might be accompanied by a student.

Another recent trend has been experimented with recently, that of a jugalbandi of an instrumentalist and a singer, notably by Ustad Bismillah Khan (shehnai) and the eminent vocalist, Girija Devi. There are no hard and fast rules for concerts, and practices have been changing with the times. Orchestral music and choral singing, though not prohibited, are not common in concerts of Hindustani classical music, primarily as they do not lend themselves to the improvisatory nature and individualistic genius of raga sangeet.

FORMAT OF A MODERN RECITAL

The format of a modern recital follows a pattern set by eminent musicians over the last seventy-five or so years. Formats have been changing in the face of technical innovations, concert venues, and the availability of time. Ustad Ali Akbar Khan was the first classical musician of repute who presented Hindustani classical music to a Western audience in New York in 1955, followed by his co-student, Pandit Ravi Shankar, the next year. Both artistes were sponsored by Yehudi Menuhin, who was singularly responsible for showcasing Indian classical music to the Western world for the first time. Although Ali Akbar's father, Ustad Allauddin Khan, had performed abroad before him, he did not have the same impact as his two students. Pandit Ravi Shankar's personal exposure to international audiences had, however, happened much earlier, when he visited the USA in 1932, at the age of twelve, as a member of his older brother Uday Shankar's dance-drama troupe. During those trips, he picked up crucial information about modern auditoria, acoustics, audience behaviour, and so on, which later came in handy when he tailored his own recitals to meet these parameters.

In India, the first conference was held at Baroda in 1916. Among the most prestigious of the concerts was the Vikramaditya Music Conference held annually at Bombay. Maharashtra has been a great centre of classical music, particularly after the shift of the film industry from Calcutta,

Lahore, and Karachi (post the India-Pakistan partition of 1947) to Bombay. Ustad Bade Ghulam Ali Khan's first major public performance was given at the Vikramaditya Conference in Bombay in 1944, in the presence of the greats of the time, notably *Aaftaab-e-Mauseeqi* (sun of music) Ustad Faiyyaz Khan of Agra. Over the next fifty years, the pattern of stage setting, sequence of presentation and progression of recitals set by doyens like Pandit Ravi Shankar, Ustad Ali Akbar Khan, and Ustad Bade Ghulam Ali Khan were emulated and became the standard in concert-style raga sangeet performances which continues till this day.

THE STAGE SETTING

The setting for a khayal recital with the full complement of musicians is along the following general pattern. In front, centre stage, facing the audience, is the main performer. Behind him or her, on either side, sit one or two tanpura accompanists (generally two for vocal and one for instrumental recitals). To the primary musician's right, inclined inwards, sits the percussion accompanist. To his left, also inclined inwards, is the instrumental accompanist (in vocal recitals only). In case the main artiste brings his disciples along as supporting singers or players, they sit in the last row, beside the tanpura players.

A complete vocal khayal recital consists of three movements. These are really stages where a performer moves from one phase of his recital to the next. Although each movement is a complete entity by itself, the three together constitute a full recital in the true sense. The three main movements are – the *alap* (prelude), the *vilambit* (slow) khayal and the *drut* (fast) khayal. Occasionally, a fourth movement might be added after the *drut* khayal in the form of a tarana. Sometimes, the performer might even replace the *drut* khayal with a tarana.

THE ALAP

The first and opening movement of a recital is the introduction of the chosen raga to the audience. This is done in the form of an alap, which is a musical prelude. The alap is a delineation of the musical structure of the raga, its pattern of notes, their sequence of use in ascent and descent, and the overall mood-emotion which it seeks to evoke. The alap is not a musical composition as such, but a freewheeling exploration of the structure of the raga. An alap may last from fifteen to thirty minutes. Although it is an introductory prelude, it is significant as it forms the musical and emotional base that sets the tone for the rest of the recital. It brings forth all the emotions that the raga seeks to evoke. It is a solemn, meditative movement which lays down the boundaries of the raga. In fact, the alap before a khayal carries the lingering influence of its predecessor, the dhrupad, and is often sung in the same way. It is the musical and emotional foundation on which the movements following it will be built.

An alap is literally an unfolding of the notes of the raga, and their interpretation by the performer. The alap is invariably sung or played in an *ati-vilambit* (extra slow) *laya*, without any percussion accompaniment, and does not follow any rhythm cycle. In fact, being a freewheeling exposition of the artiste's imagination, it has no tempo at all, or a varying tempo that the performer sets for himself. The absence of laya and taal leave the entire emphasis on the third component of raga sangeet, which is swar, allowing the performer to dwell at length on the pattern of notes that define the raga and give full expression to the entire spectrum of its emotional content. The alap brings out the various characteristics of a raga as if it were a living being – its face, complexion, eyes and smile.

The alaps for a vocal khayal and instrumental recital are nearly identical, except for some variations. In their biography, *Ustad Bade Ghulam Ali Khan: His Life and Music*, authors Malti Gilani and Quratulain Hyder describe a morning soiree performed by the singer in the rose garden of Sir S.M. Basu's house in Calcutta in the winter of 1966. The Ustad announced that he would present Raga Todi in the form of 'the opening of a rosebud into a full-blown rose'. He did this with a beautifully unfolding alap, to the great delight of the large gathering of music lovers present.

The alap uses a number of improvisatory techniques to delineate the structure of the chosen raga. These are part and parcel of the alap, which must be savoured as a whole. The *barhat* means to proceed or increase. This is done by an incremental expansion of musical notes that the performer is exploring, starting with a few and growing into larger groups. It is also called *phailaav* (to spread). *Swar vistaar* and *phirat*, which mean to delienate the notes in greater detail and to wander around (musically), are other techniques. The artiste will expand the musical phrases gradually, in increasing, elliptical patterns, as he wanders between them, here and there.

Behlawa means 'playing around' or keeping someone happily occupied. The performer will tease a note as if playing with it and with his audience, and will do this first with one note and then with two, growing into entire phrases. *Bol alap* makes use of the lyrics of the main *bandish*, in order to dramatize the effect. *Nom-tom alap* is a leftover from dhrupad gayaki, and uses imaginary, meaningless syllables like *nom*, *tom* and so on to express musical patterns. When time is of the essence in a recital, or while recording a limited duration track, the alap can be compressed into its shorter version, which is called the *aochar*. This is also an introductory prelude, but is rendered in a crisp and concise manner. Alaps are categorized in two ways: by their extent and by their nature. *Aochar alap* falls in the first category. As mentioned, it is a short introduction to the raga. It gives only a glimpse of the raga, often using the phrases from the *bandish* itself, that is to follow. An *aochar* is neither considered as complete nor as expansive as a full-fledged *vistaar alap*. The alap allows the performer to exploit the full range of his voice or instrument, which might extend up to two-and-a-half octaves.

THE BANDISH: VILAMBIT AND DRUT KHAYAL COMPOSITIONS

After the alap, the next movement is the *bandish*. The *bandish* is the 'meat' of a khayal performance. Generally, in one recital, a performer presents two separate *bandishes*, the first one in a slow tempo, and the second in a fast one. The slow *bandish* is called *vilambit* khayal. This is followed by the fast *bandish*, called *drut* khayal and forms the third movement of the recital. The *vilambit* and *drut bandishes*, though composed in the same raga, may differ from each other in every sense, in terms of the melody, lyrics, tempo, and rhythm, but will invariably convey the same *ras-bhava* and be characterized by the same distinctive *pakad* of the raga.

Each *bandish* may last up to thirty minutes or more. They are performed one after another. Often, the *vilambit* and *drut bandishes* are set to different *taals*. As such, the artiste and percussionist make a clean break for a few seconds after completing the slow *bandish* before embarking upon the fast *bandish* with its new melody, lyrics, tempo and rhythm cycle. The *vilambit* and *drut* khayals afford the artiste the fullest possible scope for displaying his mastery over the raga in slow as well as in fast tempo, while conveying its intrinsic, underlying *ras-bhava* at the same time. Generally, the end of the *drut bandish* concludes the recital.

The *bandish* is the single, most distinguishable aspect of a khayal recital. After a full introduction to the raga in all its hues has been given in the *alap*, the *bandish* seems to come spontaneously as the next step. Each *bandish* (slow and fast) begins with the opening face of the *sthayi*, which also contains the haunting *pakad* of the raga that renders it instantly recognizable. Since the *alap* was rendered without rhythm accompaniment, it is at this juncture that the tabla joins the recital for the first time. Although the *alap* is also an improvisatory movement rendered in a slow, meditative manner, it is in the *bandish* proper that the jazz-like improvizations really come into full play.

TAAN

Once the vocalist and accompanists have fully established the melodic concept of the composition and rhythmic cycle of the *bandish*, the main performer launches the recital into its improvizational phase. This takes the form of a series of sudden, eloquent musical flourishes. Each such spontaneous, on-the-spot, improvization is called a *taan*, which means 'to stretch'. A *taan* is a burst of musical energy executed at a comparatively faster speed than the main composition, between its melodic-lyrical phrases, in slow as well as in fast *bandishes*. The *taan* may be executed primarily in three ways

– without words, as open mouthed 'aaaa' singing which is called an *akar taan*; by pronouncing the names of the notes being sung, which is called *sargam* or *saakaar taan,* or by using lyrical phrases *(bols)* from the *bandish* itself, which is called *Bol taan*. A fourth technique is a leftover from the dhrupad style in whch the *taan* is executed using meaningless phonemes such as *nom, tom* etc., and is called *nom-tom taan.*

After each such improvisatory flourish, the artiste returns to the main melody. The entire *bandish* is thus a series of long or short, crisp or flowing, intricate or simple *taans,* interspersed between the lyrical phrases and melodic patterns of the *bandish* and executed within the ongoing rhythm cycle of the tabla that continues, regular and unbroken, throughout the *bandish.* *Taans* may be rendered at very fast speeds, irrespective of the ongoing laya from which they take off and, on completion, return to. Such *taans* are called *chhoot,* or shooting *taans,* which can be rendered to perfection only by a few, highly accomplished vocalists. Other *taans* are executed in a fixed *laya,* but at double the tempo of the ongoing taal cycle and are called *baraabar ki taan,* of balanced tempo, and are the more commonly rendered type of *taans.* The most attractive feature of the *bandish* is the constant interplay between swar, bol, laya and taal. While the taal provides unfailing constancy of laya, the swar flits about like a butterfly from one *taan* to another.

Tihaayi

Another attractive technique employed during the *bandish* is the *tihaayi.* A *tihaayi* involves an intricately-woven phrase, with words from the lyrics or names of the notes which is repeated three times *(tihaayi)* consecutively. The *tihaayi,* too, like the *taans,* can be launched without warning at any stage of the recital, whenever it strikes the musician's fancy, thus providing the unique quality of *upaj* or spontaneity. The *tihaayi* must, however, end exactly on the *sam* (the concept of the *sam* is explained later). In fact, nowhere does *upaj* play a more crucial role than in the *taans, meends, harkats,* and *tihaayis* of slow and fast *bandishes.* Thus, a *bandish,* besides being a melodic composition set to a fixed tempo and rhythm cycle, is also a series of energetic musical flourishes and ornamental pieces executed at random throughout its rendition. These spontaneous, on the spot improvisations are in stark contrast to the steady tempo and faultlessly executed rhythm cycle that are maintained throughout the *bandish,* which impart a unique character to Hindustani classical music.

A short, decorative piece is called a *tukda* or *cheez,* literally, piece or item. Other such colloquial terms for ornamental techniques are *khatka, mudki* and *phanda.* These musical and rhythmic flourishes are executed extempore, at the musician's and percussionist's fancy, providing that element of surprise that is so unique to raga sangeet in general and to khayal gayaki in particular. There are many other improvisatory techniques, all of which need not clutter up our description of the progress of a *bandish.* These will appear as we expand the sphere of our listening experience. *Taans* of all types, however, constitute the most unique feature of a *bandish.*

A *bandish* is composed or 'knotted up' in a specific rhythm cycle, taal, which is played by the tabla accompanist. Each taal has a specified number of beats, with the cycle starting on the first beat. This first beat is called the *sam,* meaning balanced or equal. The main performer and his accompanists, both percussive and instrumental, collectively return to the *sam* after the completion of every taal cycle. The *sam* balances every part of the recital as it progresses, regardless of the tempo it is performed at.

The taal and laya of a *drut* and *vilambit bandish* may vary, yet the *sam* will constantly fall on the first beat of the cycle, be it a taal of six, seven, eight, ten, twelve, fourteen, or sixteen beats, played in slow, medium or fast laya. In this respect, there is no scope for error, and even the slightest hint of one can ruin the recital. The unfailing constancy of the *sam* on the first beat of the taal is an enduring charm of raga sangeet that sets it completely apart from all other genres of music, including jazz.

THE TARANA

This is a unique vocal form that uses seemingly meaningless phonemes like *nom, tom, dir dir, taa, naa,* and so on. The tarana is a *bandish* separate from the *vilambit* and *drut* khayals. For all purposes, a tarana is a fast, vocal *bandish*, except that the lyrics are substituted with syllables. It generally comes after the fast khayal or occasionally, may even be used in its stead. Its use is, however, slowly dying away, though Ustad Amir Khan (1912-1974), a great master of Hindustani classical music, had successfully revived it during his lifetime. According to Khan Sahib, the phonemes used in a tarana are actually dummy words employed to convey Hindustani sargam or songs to Persian musicians, for whom the pronunciation and cultivation of flow in the sargam was difficult. Sargam is a term contrived from the names of notes of the musical scale: Sa-re-ga-ma. Tarana singing was popular in the old days, when it encouraged competitiveness between the dhrupad singer and the veena player. Some of these phonemes used in tarana singing are close, phonetically, to the veena and sitar accents.

Taranas gave vocalists the freedom to improvize. They were also much appreciated by audiences for their unique and exotic appeal. One of the greatest taranas ever recorded is in the Raga Hansadhwani by Ustad Amir Khan himself. Ustads Nazakat Ali and Salaamat Ali were also great masters of it and their tarana in Raga *Marwa* remains a favourite over half a century after it was recorded. Several younger singers, particularly those who owe allegiance to the Agra and Rampur gharanas, have taken up the art afresh with a view to restoring its place in Khayal gayaki. Once it becomes a part of vocalists' repertoire again, it is bound to redeem the popularity it enjoyed in the previous century. Tarana singing remains one of the great sub-genres of Hindustani classical music and is, in fact, a form akin to 'scat-singing' in jazz, as practised by Ella Fitzgerald in the mid-twentieth century. Scat singing was a sub-genre popularized by the famous trumpeter, singer and composer, Louis 'Satchmo' Armstrong, though no doubt it must have been practised even earlier in New Orleans and other centres of American jazz. It is described as 'jazz singing, using sounds imitating instruments instead of words'. A modern exponent of this style is the highly talented, eight-time Grammy winner, singer, guitarist, and composer, George Benson ('Nature Boy'). He was honoured by President Bill Clinton, an amateur jazz saxophonist himself, with an invitation to perform at the White House. When Benson sings scat, he produces vocal sounds like the guitar, along with his guitar playing, note by note, till it becomes difficult to distinguish one from the other.

To summarize, the introductory alap is the first and opening movement of a khayal recital. This is followed by the *vilambit* khayal, a *bandish* composition in slow tempo. Finally, the *ðrut* khayal, a *banðish* in fast tempo which is the third and last movement. Sometimes, the last movement may be followed by a tarana or even be replaced by it.

10

Accompaniment in Raga Sangeet Recitals

Accompaniment in raga sangeet is provided by two means – instrumental and percussive. Instrumental accompaniment is usually provided only with vocal recitals, when an instrumentalist accompanies the vocalist. In an instrumental recital, if the main performer is being supported by others on the same instrument, as happens often in shehnai recitals, it is not considered accompaniment. Similarly, if a vocalist plays the harmonium while singing, he plays only a few chords or dominant notes of the raga to provide tonal support to himself, which is also not true accompaniment. True musical accompaniment to vocal khayal recitals is provided primarily by two instruments, viz, the sarangi and the harmonium. Moreover, they are played by specialists who are not only highly experienced in the classical genre itself but are consummate artistes of their instruments as well.

Instrumental accompaniment is dictated by tradition. In the northern regions of Punjab, Uttar Pradesh, Delhi, and Rajasthan, accompaniment is generally provided by the sarangi. In the Maharashtrian and North Karnataka and Konkan regions, the harmonium is the preferred choice. Bengal, though a great repository of raga sangeet, did not have its own gharanas and remained an extension of the UP and Awadhi tradition due to the historical events of the nineteenth century, with happy results. Both the sarangi and the harmonium are equally popular in Bengal as accompanying instruments.

INSTRUMENTAL ACCOMPANIMENT

The Tanpura

The tanpura, strictly speaking, is not an instrument for accompaniment in the manner of the sarangi or the harmonium. It is a unique device that produces an unmatched, continuous drone of tonal resonance, which forms a backdrop for the main artiste's music. The tanpura provides a veritable canvas for the performer to paint a portrait of the chosen raga. In a full-fledged vocal concert or recording performance, two tanpuras are played by a pair of musicians seated behind the singer, providing a continuous pitch. Some singers like to play one themselves while they sing. Both are acceptable, though neither is considered true instrumental accompaniment.

The tanpura is widely used in all kinds of music, and provides the single most important point of concentration for the musician, particularly a vocalist. It is a long-necked lute, attached to a balloon shaped echo chamber (made of a dried gourd) at the bottom, which is called the *tumba*. The instrument has a total length of three to five feet. On the front face of the neck four strings are mounted. The two strings in the middle are known as the *joda* (pair) and are tuned to the middle *sa*. The first string is tuned to the lower *pa*, while the fourth and last one, which is also the thickest, made of brass or coiled, is tuned to the lowest *sa*. There are no frets in the tanpura, and its strings are played open or blank with one hand. The first string is always played with the middle finger and the rest with the index finger. It is said that when the four strings are plucked in succession continuously, their droning, resonating sounds at the four pitches mentioned above, merge into one another, forming an 'aural rainbow.' To hear the rich drone of twin tanpuras resonating without respite behind a singer, particularly during the perceivable gaps between his spontaneous musical flourishes, is a treat in itself.

Swarmandal

As already mentioned, the practice of self-accompaniment on the harmonium does not fall within the ambit of instrumental accompaniment. Similarly, there is a one-of-a-kind musical device for self-accompaniment of such sonorous beauty that it demands particular mention here, even though it too does not fulfill the requirement of true instrumental accompaniment, in the manner of the sarangi or the harmonium. This unique instrument is the swarmandal.

Also called surmandal in common parlance, this instrument became popular among vocalists during the latter half of the twentieth century. Before that, it was used only by a few, the first among them being Ustad Bade Ghulam Ali Khan, followed by Begum Akhtar, and the brothers, Nazaakat Ali and Salaamat Ali. It produces the most exquisite and mellifluous sound, unlike any other musical device. Its strings may vary in number from around twenty-one to thirty-six, but are generally fixed at twenty-eight by maestros. They are tuned to the scale of the raga the instrument is accompanying, and some strings may need to be re-tuned for another raga.

The swarmandal is held upright in the lap, resting against the torso of the singer, who strums on it at irregular intervals to light up the scale, as it were. Sometimes he might softly touch upon just a few strings tuned to the dominant notes of the raga, and at other times, may run through the entire spectrum in long, unhurried strokes, as the fancy strikes him. Some singers put it flat on their folded legs, facing upwards.

The swarmandal is not of Indian origin, but is begotten from the Psaltery of ancient Palestine, which King David is said to have played while composing Biblical Psalms. In the Arabic tradition, King David's singing is referred to as *Lehr-e-Dawoodi*. In Palestine, the psaltery is called *Barbath* and can be seen in murals and frescoes of Grecian and Roman antiquity.

It is nothing short of a miracle that one of the greatest singers of all time, Ustad Bade Ghulam Ali Khan, a veritable king of music himself, was to discover an old, unused psaltery in a junk shop in Lahore in 1914 or 1915. He was then in his early teens, and could not afford to pay its cost of five rupees. Since the shopkeeper knew his family, he allowed him to take the psaltery and pay for it in installments later. The boy took it home, polished it till it shone, strung it up, and tuned it to the twelve-note scale. He christened the new instrument he had adapted as swarmandal, literally, a gathering of notes.

It is now a staple for many singers, notably the two current stars, Ustad Rashid Khan and Pandit Ajoy Chakraborty. As in the case of the tanpura, the swarmandal is also not considered an instrument of true accompaniment.

Sarangi

The sarangi is an instrument of musical accompaniment in the true sense of the term. It is a highly melodious instrument that comes closest to the human voice in terms of continuity of sound and tonal modulation. In my view, there is nothing the human voice can produce which the sarangi cannot exactly replicate. The sarangi is the classical adaptation of an ancient folk instrument, the *Ravan-hathha*, believed to have been played by Ravan, King of Lanka in the epic, Ramayana. It is still used in its original form by the Langas and Manganiyars, tribes of minstrels who live in the Thar Desert.

The sarangi is also one of the most difficult and physically challenging instruments to play. It has three main playing strings tuned to *sa, pa,* and (upper) *sa,* with another thirty-five-odd sympathetic strings that are called *tarab.* Sympathetic strings are not played but resonate by themselves when the main ones are played or struck. Sound is produced when the player plays the main strings with a bow, made of gut or horsehair, with one hand. With the other hand, he slides his fingertips on the finger-board but, unlike all other stringed instruments, does not press on the strings from the top. Instead, his fingernails graze against the string from the side, producing the note corresponding to the point on the string where the nail touches it. As a result, most sarangi players suffer broken nails or damaged cuticles, and often require them to be lubricated before playing.

The sarangi is held upright in the lap, with its neck resting on the player's left shoulder. It has a short, fretless finger-board, about twelve to fourteen inches high, on which the player slides his left hand with fast and continuous up-and-down movements, grazing the string with his fingernails from the side. Simultaneously, he plays the strings with the bow in his right hand.

As an accompanist, the sarangi player follows the singer, and replicates exactly what he sings while remaining two or three notes behind the latter. He might play continuously in this 'follow-the-singer' technique, or may leave short gaps at intervals of his own choosing. Sarangi styles, like the rest of Hindustani classical music, differ from one gharana to another. Yet both the vocalist and the accompanist invariably come together at the *jam*. The *jam* is that all commanding moment in Hindustani classical music, when all three, swar, taal and laya come together in a resounding crescendo.

For a variety of reasons, including difficulty in playing the instrument and the lack of demand, the numbers of good sarangi players is dwindling by the day. In the 1980s, some of them led by the young Dhruba Ghosh had teamed up to provide a boost to this melodic and majestic instrument, a project which even got them a cover story in the magazine, *India Today*. Hopefully, we will see sarangi players of the calibre of the brothers Pandits Hanuman and Gopal Prasad Mishra, Pandit Ram Narain and Ustad Sultan Khan once again. In my opinion, an authentic, high-class vocal *khayal* recital is incomplete without the sarangi. One only needs to listen to the recordings of Ustad Bade Ghulam Ali Khan and his son, Ustad Munawwar Ali Khan, or modern maestros like Ustad Rashid Khan and Pandit Ajoy Chakraborty, to experience the magic of the sarangi.

Music composer Khayyam used the sarangi to perfection in an album of ghazals by Begum Akhtar in the 1970s, an exercise he repeated for Muzaffar Ali in his film, *Umrao Jaan* and won a Filmfare Award for it.

Harmonium

This is also an instrument for true accompaniment. The choice of sarangi for accompaniment vis-à-vis the harmonium is a matter of tradition. The technique of harmonium accompaniment in a vocal recital is identical to the one followed by sarangi players. They too, follow the singer, keeping two or three notes behind. The versatility and tonal qualities of the two instruments are, however, markedly unequal. The sarangi is a highly sophisticated musical device before which the harmonium pales in comparison. As an instrument for self-accompaniment, however, the harmonium is invaluable.

Microtones cannot be played on any keyboard instrument including the harmonium. As a matter of historical detail, according to Pandit Ajoy Chakraborty, the development of the harmonium in its present form (for use in raga sangeet) is attributed to Dwarkanath Ghosh, the grandfather of the great twentieth century musician and teacher, Pandit Gyan Prakash Ghosh, and is known as the *Dwarkin harmonium*.[5]

Another interesting fact pertains to a unique harmonium designed by an Englishman, H. Keatly Moore, in 1910. He was a keen lover of Indian music and specially developed this instrument that could play the full twenty-two note Indian microtonic scale called *shruti*. For some reason, this microtonic harmonium did not catch the fancy of the musical fraternity and became extinct within a decade of Moore's death. Nevertheless, as an instrument for accompanying vocal music, the standard harmonium occupies a special place in Hindustani classical music and many singers cannot sing without its accompaniment.

PERCUSSION ACCOMPANIMENT: THE TABLA

Percussive accompaniment for dhrupad gayaki used to be provided (and still is) by the *pakhawaj* but for khayal recitals, it is invariably provided by the tabla. Generally, in vocal recitals, tabla accompaniment is kept simple and straightforward, devoid of undue ornamentation. Since vocal music is the bedrock of raga sangeet, the singer's artistry must be the centrepiece of the recital. Therefore the tabla provides only the rhythmic framework within which the vocalist creates his melodic improvizations. However in instrumental recitals, the *tabalchi or tabaliya* plays a more prominent part, coming almost at par with the main instrumentalist. Both together provide an interesting display of cooperation, and even work towards providing a counterpoint to the other.

THE SAM

The *sam* is the first beat of a rhythm cycle, whatever be the number of beats that constitute the cycle or whichever tempo it is played at. As explained earlier, the *sam* plays a central role in regulating rhythm cycles and maintaining laya patterns in Hindustani classical music in all its sub-genres. All accompanying participants in a recital, led by the tabla player, return to the *sam* together after completion of the rhythm cycle. If, however, the main artiste (vocalist or instrumentalist) embarks on a musical perambulation that spans two or more cycles of the taal being played, he may not always physically return to the *sam* at the end of each and every taal cycle, but will invariably acknowledge it while passing through it. The end of his perambulation, whatever its length might be, will coincide exactly with the *sam*. Sometimes, the instrumentalist's melodic phrases are replied to by the tabalchi with matching percussive phrases, a practice that is called rather appropriately *sawaal-jawaab* (question and answer). This is one of the many techniques the performer and his percussion accompanist employ to engage the audience's interest throughout the recital. Each question and answer will invariably end on the sam.

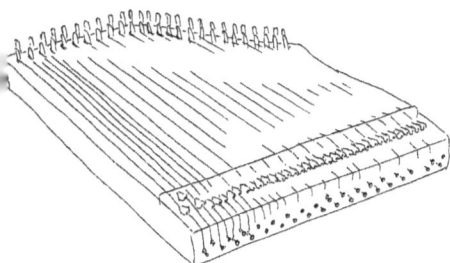

11

Format of an Instrumental Recital

Movements of an instrumental recital are similar to the general pattern of a khayal recital described earlier. This includes an alap, followed by two *bandishes* in slow and fast tempi respectively. However, over a period of time, minor variations have come about in the instrumental khayal, primarily in the alap, which have gained currency among musicians and listeners alike. This is especially so in sitar and sarod recitals, due to the over-arching influence of three distinguished instrumentalists who formed the 'musical triumvirate' in the mid-twentieth century – Ustad Ali Akbar Khan (sarod), Pandit Ravi Shankar, and Ustad Vilayat Khan (both sitar). These variations, though slight, become significant when we consider the immense popularity of instrumental music, in live and recorded performances alike. Since the beginner is advised to start his journey by listening to instrumental music, it is vitally important that he is able to follow every part of an instrumental recital perfectly.

Instrumental music recitals, particularly sitar and sarod, have developed a distinct character of their own. The immense popularity of these instruments among audiences has resulted in some instrumentalists achieving iconic status. This was particularly so in the case of the famous triumvirate mentioned above. It remains so among the leading players of today, notably Ustad Amjad Ali Khan (sarod), Ustad Shahid Parvez and Pandit Budhaditya Mukherjee (both sitar) along with a host of other upcoming instrumentalists like Purbayan Chatterji. The movements of a sitar or sarod recital, though theoretically the same as those of a vocal recital, have some minor movements of their own.

A sitar or sarod recital commences with an alap. The alap in all instrumental recitals serves the same introductory purpose as it does in a vocal one, and is identical in execution to the latter. For sitar and sarod recitals, however, there are two additional mini-movements, which are called *jod* and *jhala*. *Jod* is a mini-movement peculiar to sitar and sarod recitals. It literally means to join. In this case, *jod* joins the alap to the *bandish* that follows it. Like the alap, the jod, too, has no rhythm or *taal* accompaniment. However, the sitarist or *sarodiya* develops a distinct laya of his own, unaided by percussion, which gradually increases as it progresses. The performer displays his artistry by running through the entire scale of the raga, improvising from the lower to the higher octave, back and forth, as in a vocal alap.

The *jhala* is also a mini-movement peculiar to sitar and sarod recitals. It follows the *jod*, almost as an extension of the latter, but at an even faster tempo, though still without any percussion accompaniment. The *jod* and *jhala* are exemplifications of the artiste's virtuosity in solo-playing. A unique feature of the *jhala* is the employment of the *chikaari* string, which is the last string in the sitar or sarod, which the player plucks at regular intervals for the purpose of improvising laya patterns, called *layakari*, which is a characteristic of this movement. The *jhala* continues to increase in tempo as it progresses, ending in a flourish at the self created *sam*. It may be fair to say that the alap, jod and *jhala*, taken together, are the instrumentalist's solo warm-up before he commences the *bandish*.

PERCUSSION ACCOMPANIMENT

After the rhythm-less alap, *jod* and *jhala* have ended, the instrumentalist begins the *vilambit bandish* in slow tempo. He does this by improvising elongated and circuitous opening phrases called *uthaan* or uthaav (rising). Simultaneously, the tabla player joins in for the first time in the recital, also with an extended flourish of tabla bols called *peshkaar* (presentation). The opening phrases of the instrumentalist, along with the introductory tabla *bols*, signal the start of the *bandish*. (The *uthaan* or rising described above has been dubbed the 'Rousing' by the renowned, veteran *tabalchi*, Pandit Shankar Ghosh, while alluding in a humorous vein, to those listeners who may have dozed off during a long, rhythmless alap).

The instrumentalist's uthaan and the *tabalchi's peshkaar* invariably end on the *sam*, thereby enhancing the instrumentalist-percussionist partnership. Thereafter, the two commence the main *bandish*, the instrumentalist with his *sthaayi* and the percussionist with the selected rhythm cycle. Once the basic melody, rhythm and tempo of the *bandish* are established, the instrumentalist commences the improvisatory phase and the recital proceeds in much the same way as a vocal performance, with all the ornamental techniques like *taans, tihaayis, meend,* and *gamak*. The uthaan and *peshkaar* are used in all types of instrumental recitals, when commencing a *bandish* with tabla accompaniment after conclusion of the rhythm-less *alap*.

While in a vocal recital, the slow and fast *bandishes* are called *vilambit* and *drut* khayal, respectively, in instrumental recitals, they are called *vilambit* and *drut Gat*. A khayal is the imagination of the performer, which consists of the melodic composition as well as its lyrical poetry. Since there are no lyrics in the instrumental version, the khayal becomes *gat* (from *gati*, which means movement or tempo). Other than the absence of lyrics in the latter, the two movements are similar.

Ever since Lord Yehudi Menuhin's presentation of India's ancient musical tradition to foreign audiences in the mid-1950s, our classical music, particularly its instrumental version, has achieved international acclaim. It becomes, therefore, that much more significant for new listeners to grasp the basic format, musical content and the interplay between melody and percussion of an instrumental recital to the fullest extent possible. Moreover, in the absence of the spotlight focusing almost entirely on the main performer (as in the case of vocal recitals) the rewards of audience appreciation are shared equally between the instrumentalist and the percussionist. The element of ornamentation, so central to Hindustani classical music, also plays a very major role in instrumental recitals. As already mentioned elsewhere, the beginner is advised to commence his journey with instrumental music.

12

Fusion Music

A relatively new concept – fusion music – has been making inroads into the secluded world of Hindustani classical music. Uninformed listeners often get taken in by this concept, which might often be nothing more than gimmickry. A *rasik* should be able to separate the grain from the chaff. To this end, I have tried to explain the possibilities and limitations of fusion music and its feasibility or futility. Recent experiments in this field have led to a happy development: a new trend known as Lounge Music. This trend has attracted many listeners with its seductive sounds and innovative recording techniques. With newer technologies becoming available every year, music in general and classical music (Western as well as Indian) in particular, is struggling to retain the attention of young people all over the world. Lounge music is one such part of the struggle.

As the name suggests, fusion music represents a coming together, musically, of different traditions. Genuine fusion would be true to its name only if it was among equals, bringing together the optimum genius of their respective musical genres to the joint effort. This has not really been achieved so far. Attempts have been made earlier between the two great traditions, starting with Yehudi Menuhin and Pandit

Ravi Shankar (Pandit Kanai Dutt on the tabla) over sixty years ago; and jazz guitarist James McLaughlin and classical violinist Dr L. Subramaniam among others, more recently. Major problem areas remain, which are enumerated below:-

If Hindustani Classical Music as high art is to 'fuse' with another genre of equal sophistication, the full classicism of *both* must come into play. However, except for the simplest, most rudimentary eight beat (4-4) *kehrwa taal*, no other *taal* has been attempted in what is passed off as Fusion Music. This is so primarily because no other musical tradition possesses music that could possibly fuse with any other of our Hindustani music *taal* cycles. Western musical emphasis has always been on melody, harmony and symphonic compositions. Wherever rhythm is incorporated, it is mainly as waltzes and minuets. In light of the prerequisites for true fusion mentioned above, such a forced fusion between two incompatibles makes for an unequal music. The only two old traditions of acknowledged musical sophistication are Western Classical and Indian Classical music. Eminent musicologists of both traditions generally agree that pure Western Classical Music and its pure Indian counterpart cannot fuse, as the former is wholly formalized while the latter, entirely improvizational. This truism was perceived by Lord Yehudi Menuhin and Pandit Ravi Shankar themselves when they experimented with fusion over half a century ago. That is why it was never repeated.

One wonders whether it is the musicians who are fusing or is it their music? It appears that whatever goes around as Fusion Music today is not really a fusion of two musical traditions but that of two musicians, belonging to different traditions, 'jamming' together. Moreover, one of them is invariably diluting his art to come level with the other. The scholar-musician, Pandit Ravi Shankar gives his frank opinion in an All India Radio archival documentary film, as follows:

'Experiments should not be done just for their own sake but for specific purposes like fusion programmes or films, both for commercial and documentary purposes. Perforce, it (the Indian component) is not and should not be called Hindustani classical music. Nor is it meant to be. It is just an experiment.'

NEW TRENDS: LOUNGE MUSIC

Thankfully, the above truth has prevailed and is now acknowledged by musicians, both classical and popular alike. The emerging trend is towards a new kind of music, composed and performed by talented musicians, well versed in the classical genre. They produce high quality 'light music' for high quality listening pleasure. Their target audience is one that appreciates good music, though not necessarily of a pure classical pedigree. The results have been very heartening. Modern electronics, keyboards, bass, brass and woodwinds are being included with sitar, sarod, santoor, and tabla in a rapidly mutating environment. This is a well advised change from the earlier, half-baked attempts at fusion music (though some musicians continue to persist with the latter, primarily to pamper a generation of high-spending ignoramuses.) This new, high quality music has been given the very appropriate generic name, 'lounge music.' The aim, as it has revealed itself so far, appears to be neither to fuse the un-fusable nor to dilute one to accommodate the other but to genuinely create a new style, if not a genre, by taking the best from each tradition.

In lounge music, pop, raga sangeet, jazz, *sufiaana kalaam* et al have been brought together by trained musicians and recorded by professional recordists. Among its earliest pioneers were Dr L. Subramaniam and his brother L. Shankar (as the band, *Shakti,* along with guitarist John McLaughlin); Louis Banks' group *Silk,* (with whom Shankar Mahadevan sang earlier) has also performed with Pandit Hari Prasad Chaurasia and Ustad Sabir Khan (tabla), among others; Pandits Shiv Kumar Sharma and Hari Prasad Chaurasia (as *Shiv-Hari*) composed excellent music for the film *Silsila* and Hariharan and Leslie Lewis came together as *The Colonial Cousins* to give us some superlative music.

The highly talented duo of the Wadali brothers, traditional singers of *naatiya kalaam,* a qawwali-like, north Indian folk mode, have recently been roped in by Times Music for a lounge music album entitled *Yaad Piya Ki.* New experimenters are also achieving great success as we see in the work of the now successful film music directors Shankar-Ehsaan-Loy, sitarist Purbayan Chatterjee and his *Shastriya Syndicate* and Abhijit Pohankar to name a few. Happily, many more are waiting in the wings.

Lounge Music is nothing but light or 'westernized' semi-classical Indian music by another name. It uses raga-based melodies and basic rhythm patterns, played on Indian as well as Western instruments by professionally trained musicians, using high end recording techniques. When an audience gets hooked on to such high class, soft-classical music, the more musically-aesthetically inclined among them start craving for the real, hard-core stuff. That is how *rasiks* are born.

13

Enjoying, Appreciating and Understanding Hindustani Classical Music

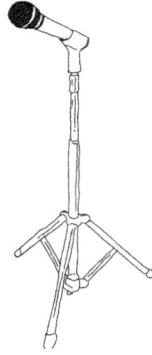

Ustad Amjad Ali Khan has often said that one should not try to 'understand' raga sangeet, but to 'perceive' it. Being an aesthetic experience, it needs to be felt by the heart, rather than be comprehended by the mind. We must, therefore, arrive at a methodology to achieve what we set out to do, that is, enjoy, appreciate and understand Hindustani classical music, in that order.

Having discussed the theoretical aspects, we will take the next, logical step. Like any other field of endeavour, the best method for achieving success is practice, practice and more practice. In our context, this translates into listening, listening, and more listening. Pandit Ajoy Chakraborty also emphasizes the need for informed audience participation in his book, *Shrutinandan* mentioned above. 'The audience should acquire some basic knowledge about significant aspects of classical music such as the twelve-note system, rhythm and tempo to gain an aesthetic and sublime experience. One can also wholeheartedly practise listening to such music.'

The more you experience, the more you enjoy it. One place to hear good raga sangeet is at concerts. We have seen what going to a concert entails and what we can hope to find there. However, concerts that showcase high quality music, performed by established musicians, are hard to come by, except in the metropolitan cities. Most shows start at six in the evening, and not everyone, particularly young professionals, can make it to the hall in time. Moreover, one evening's concert might feature three or four artistes, not all of whom may be our first listening choice. It may not be worth the time and money to spend an entire evening listening to three or four performers when only one of them, who is hopefully not the last, is the reason for our venturing there. For beginners, especially, it is of paramount importance to attain and sustain the element of joy. In order to achieve this, we must endeavour to listen to what pleases us the most, thereby enhancing and optimizing our enjoyment.

Twenty-five years ago, one could find a collection of good recordings of raga sangeet only in a few music shops, and that too in big cities. The situation has changed vastly, and CDs are now available almost everywhere – at airports, hotels, bus stands, and tourist destinations. Excellent music is available on YouTube too, which affords the beginner a wide listening choice that he can exercise to make his journey of discovery a pleasant and fruitful one.

With a little guidance from friends, knowledgeable staff of large stores, or owners of music shops, the beginner can locate the right mix of music to listen to. The more you listen, the easier it becomes to identify and gradually recognize ragas which, though not *de rigueur*, enhances one's listening pleasure. This is what music appreciation is all about. Dust jackets of most CDs contain valuable information about the musician and the music. These should be read through. The beginner must try and identify the *taal* which the accompanying percussionist is playing, and follow it while listening. To start with, doing so might be easier in light or semi-classical music, which employ simpler *taal* cycles. Finally, the beginner must try and identify the *sam* and anticipate its arrival throughout the recital. Being able to do so will greatly help him get involved with what he is listening to. These are the first steps towards becoming a *rasik*. The rest will come on its own, over a period of time.

In all this, we must never forget that we are pursuing a hobby of our choice, of our own volition. It is not a study course that has to be got over and done with as fast as possible. It is a lifelong relationship between the *rasik* and his muse. The hallmark of such a relationship is ardent, sincere and heartfelt devotion.

Appreciation albums are a noble effort made by some respected musicians with a view to ensuring the wellbeing of raga sangeet. However, in my opinion, such albums cannot be starting points for beginners who might be venturing into Hindustani classical music for the first time. They are, however, invaluable for those who have already achieved a measure of basic grounding in raga sangeet.

Certain clubs and music lovers' societies who organize music concerts, also offer music appreciation classes to their members, which are helpful for beginners. All these aids have their place in the would-be *rasik's* journey of discovery. Nothing, however, comes close to practice, practice, and yet more practice, except listening, listening, and yet more listening.

'The pulse of India throbs in the music and the dance-drama. It is in the realm of living that India exposes herself, without consciousness. The poetry, the stoicism in face of aching tragedy, the austere discipline of the yogi, the languishing air of over-rich beauty, the heaviness of joss-stick perfume... all these are India. The plaintive shepherd's flute surging across forbidding Himalayan valleys; a wandering Rajasthani minstrel intoning an hour-long ballad, carrying with him the breath of the Middle Ages...'

These excerpts from *The Music of India* by Peggy Holroyd illustrate a Western observer's view of the real strengths of India They have been specially quoted rather than those of an Indian, as the latter could be explained away as the exhortations of a jingo-nationalist. Among all its strengths, the pull of the music of India is the strongest. What could be better than going on a journey to its heart?

14

The World of Rhythm Percussion in Hindustani Classical Music

IMPORTANCE OF RHYTHM

Although percussion is generally considered a mode of accompaniment of the singer or instrumentalist, in Hindustani classical music the percussionist's contribution is far more than that. Among all the musical traditions of the world, no genre lays so much emphasis on rhythm as does Indian music in general and raga sangeet in particular. Western music has two basic rhythm cycles, viz the 1-2, 1-2 beat of the foxtrot/quickstep and the 1-2-3, 1-2-3 beat of the waltz. All other exotic rhythms such as tango, samba, rumba, cha cha cha, and bossa nova are not rhythm cycles but dances, accompanied by rhythms that are basically variants of the first, 1-2, 1-2 beat. The classical music of India, on the other hand, uses such a vast and varied array of rhythm cycles as to render any comparison with its Western counterpart redundant. The over-arching emphasis in Western classical music is on melody and harmony, as testified by their prodigious treasure trove of great symphonic works.

The culture of north India uses rhythm in all forms of music and dance, classical, semi-classical, light or folk. An informed listener must understand the rudiments of the *taal* cycles commonly used in Hindustani classical music in order to appreciate a recital in its entirety. Merely being told by the announcer that, 'the following *bandish* is set to *teen taal*, a cycle of sixteen beats' is meaningless. The listener must know exactly how those 16 beats are organized, how many chambers they are broken up into and where the accent within each chamber lies. In short, he should be able to identify the *taal* himself and thereafter, follow it from *sam* to *sam*. This chapter discusses percussion in Indian music and explains the common *taal* cycles used in raga sangeet and the basic bols (rhythm lyrics) of each.

THE HISTORY OF RHYTHM INSTRUMENTS

The oldest percussion instrument is considered to be the pakhawaj. According to Hindu mythology, it was created and first played by Lord Shiva himself. The mythological name for the pakhawaj is mridang (in the Carnatic tradition, mridangam, which though smaller in size is similar to the pakhawaj). In Carnatic music, the mridangam continues to be the main percussion instrument. Till the eighteenth century, the pakhawaj was the main instrument for rhythm accompaniment to North Indian raga sangeet too. The tabla, the main percussion instrument today, originates from the pakhawaj. Though the name tabla comes from the Arabic *tab'l* (drum, as in tab'l-e-jung or battle drums), the instrument itself is entirely of Indian origin.

Till the mid-eighteenth century when *dhrupad* was the principal singing style, rhythm was provided by the pakhawaj. Although historical accounts are vague, the pakhawaj gave way to the tabla around the same time as the khayal was evolving from the *dhrupad*, during the reign of the later Mughals. There is a mistaken belief that the tabla too, is an invention of the thirteenth century poet-musician, Amir Khusrau, whereas it actually evolved almost 500 years later. This confusion stems from the fact that at the court of the colourful king, Mohammad Shah *Rangeele*, there was another musician by the name of Khusrau Khan, who conceived the tabla pair from the single pakhawaj.

A few years later another court musician, Siddhaar Khan, gave the tabla its final form, i.e. with a circular patch of black paste in the middle of both drums. Currently, the black patch in the centre of each drum is made from a mixture of powdered rice and scrap-iron dust, applied delicately, layer upon layer, to get the desired result. It would be fair to surmise that the evolution of khayal and tabla are contemporaneous and that both evolved (from the dhrupad and pakhawaj respectively) under the aegis of the colourful king in the mid-eighteenth century. The tabla, though grammatically singular is actually a pair of drums, as if a pakhawaj had been halved in two. The left-hand drum is called the *baayaan* (left) and the right-hand drum, the *daanyaan* (right). They correspond to the left face of the pakhawaj which emits a deep, bass sound; and its right face which has a sharper, higher pitch. By halving the pakhawaj, this contrast in pitch was further accentuated and a unique pair of drums, the tabla was born, one with a deep resonance and the other, with a crisp sharpness.

A tabla player sitting cross-legged on the floor with his drums at each knee, finds his hands coming to rest naturally on the upturned faces of the two drums. He then plays them with both hands with the greatest ease, using his fingers (tips, knuckles, and nails), palms (partly or fully open) and base of the hand or wrist, to provide an endless array of rhythmic sounds at various speeds. Due to its tautness, the right hand *daanyaan* is the main drum which produces a variety of *taal* patterns, while the resonant, left hand *baanyaan* provides the bass sounds as a background to the former.

The tabla, like all other instruments, also requires to be tuned. The right drum is tuned to middle *sa*, by adjusting the leather lashings around it with the help of a small hammer, thus tightening or loosening the skin of its surface to achieve the desired pitch. Similarly, the left drum is tuned to the lower sa. Together, the tabla pair forms a unique percussion instrument, nonpareil in any musical tradition. Its intonations are exact to its sounds and, in musical notation, are written likewise. It is the most innovative and communicative of all the drums of the world.

The tabla is a percussion instrument that carries the *taal* or rhythm cycle to which a *bandish* is set. The *taal* cycle is spelt out by its notations, which are called bols or lyrics of the tabla. These lyrics describe the various sounds that the two drums, singly or jointly, produce such as ta, na, dha, tin, dhin, etc. A complete rhythm cycle, from its first beat or *sam* and return thereto, is called the *Theka* of that *taal*. The *theka* provides the backbone to the recital through each movement of its presentation, i.e., the slow and fast khayals. It lays down the all important *sam*, to which the main artiste and his accompanist (sarangi or harmonium) must repeatedly and consistently return, irrespective of their individual melodic or percussive excursions.

TABLA GHARANAS

Like the gharana system enumerated earlier, the tabla also has its gharanas, differing from one another in their styles of playing and emphasis on different facets of percussion. Briefly, there are two main styles of tabla playing: The *Dilli baaj* or Delhi style which evolved since the inception of the tabla in the mid-eighteenth century and the *Poorab baaj*, which developed later in Eastern (*poorab*) India, after the demise of the Mughal empire. *Dilli baaj* is characterized by its distinctive bols created from the edge of the right hand *∂aanyaan* with the index and middle fingers of the hand. *Poorab baaj* developed primarily in present day Uttar Pradesh. The tabla gharanas that play in this style are named after Benaras, Lucknow, Rampur, and Farakkabad-Ajrada, erstwhile pricipalities located in this region to which musicians migrated in the eighteenth-nineteenth century after the break up of the Mughal Empire. These gharanas have distinctly varying styles of playing. The Benaras style lays greater emphasis on deep, resonant sound effects originating from the left hand drum or *baanyaan*. In fact, Pandit Shamta Prasad, one of the stalwarts of this gharana was nicknamed *Go∂aayi* Maharaj for his scintillating left-hand work on the *baanyaan* (which he held in his lap or 'gode', hence *go∂aayi*). Similarly, Ustad Karamatulla Khan of Farakkabad/Rampur was famous for the elegance of his right hand work on the *∂aanyaan*, as was Ustad Ahmed Jaan 'Thirakwa' of the same gharana.

Another tabla gharana also evolved in the form of the *Punjabi* gharana. This is a later development and reached its pinnacle in the person of Ustad Allah Rakkha Qureshi (1919-2000), a musician of stupendous artistry and elegant sophistication, among others of lesser renown. Obviously, this gharana too grew out of the original *Dilli baaj*, as did all the others, but developed in Northwest India (including what is now Pakistan.) Its present custodian is the late Ustad's son, Zakir Hussain, a highly gifted percussionist who has added much to his illustrious father's legacy. These gharanas no longer exist in their originally exclusive forms and the tabla is now played in a more or less composite style, though many artistes retain the distinctive characteristics of the regional *baaj* they follow.

OTHER DRUMS OF NORTH INDIA

Besides the pakhawaj and the tabla, the other major drum is the dholak, a pakhawaj lookalike but shorter in length and without paste on its faces and much lesser in tonal range. The dholak is the main instrument for folk music and dance. It has achieved wide acclaim as rhythm accompaniment for *qawwali* singing, a choral form of Urdu poetry. Another drum pair is the naqqaara (nagaara in common parlance). These are a pair of shallow drums of varying sizes played with drumsticks. The larger ones were used as war-drums in the past (dating as far back to Alexander's invasion in 326 BCE) and the smaller ones are used to accompany the shehnai, a familiar sight at any Indian festive occasion. Though the naqqaara is traditionally played with drumsticks, for classical shehnai recitals, it has been adapted for playing with the hands like the tabla. Every old palace-fortress in the North Indian subcontinent has a platform above the gate or on either side of the main entrance to its forecourt known as the naqqar khaana where the naqqara players sat and played to welcome the royal master or his guests in bygone days. Yet another type of drum is the Dhol, a large, barrel-shaped drum favoured by farming communities in North India to celebrate the harvest and other folk festivals. Strung around the neck, it is played with sticks in a standing position, often accompanying the Bhangra dance of Punjab. In Rajasthan, where folk music often approaches the level of high art, the humble dhol is used to produce a dazzling variety of intricate rhythms for music and dance, particularly in the areas of Jodhpur and Bikaner, geographically referred to as Marwar.

Taal Cycles: Organization of a Cycle

Rhythm (*taal*) is the measurement of a fixed time lag. This measurement is done by breaking up that time lag into divisions, which are called matras or beats. Thus, when a fixed time lag is divided into sixteen matras, it is called a 16 beat cycle, if into six, then a six beat cycle and so on. These matras or beats are then grouped into 'chambers', called *khands*. *Teen taal* is a cycle of sixteen beats, which are grouped into four *khands* of four matras each. These 16 beats in four khands, are notated thus: 4-4-4-4. However, all these four *khands* are not similar; one *khand* is distinguished from the other by designating whether it will have a 'clap' (taalee) or a 'blank' (*khaalee*) in it. These claps and blanks divide the *taal* cycle into comprehensible frames and identify its progress as it proceeds from *sam* to *sam*. *Matras* or beats are not just mechanical repetitions. Each beat has its own distinctive sound. The sounds of each beat are enunciated by ascribing words to them, just like lyrics to a melody.

For instance, a single strike on the ege of the daanyaan is *tin*, whereas when this is played along with a strike on the baanyaan, both together produce the sound *dhin*. A full *taal* cycle is described by reciting all its bols, consisting of *matras*, taalees, *khaalees* and the *sam*. A full cycle thus laid down is called the *theka* or basic rhythm pattern of that *taal*. This will be better understood when we discuss some major *taals* in Hindustani classical music and, of course, by listening to raga sangeet over a period of time.

LAYA AND TAAL

Laya (tempo) is the gap between one *maatra* and the next, in the same, fixed time lag. A long gap denotes a slow tempo and a short gap, a fast tempo. However, laya remains relevant even when there are no beats being played, as in the alap, where a musician creates his own voice-tempo. If sixteen matras are played in a given time lag, it lays down a certain laya or tempo. If this laya is doubled, perforce there will be thirty-two beats within that same time lag. Similarly, if the laya is halved, only eight beats will be played. Hence, the same *taal* can be played in different layas, slow, medium, and fast. Slow tempo is called *vilambit* laya, medium, madhya laya, and fast, *drut* laya. To designate the 'extra' slow or fast, the suffix 'ati' is used, as in *ati-vilambit* or *ati-drut*. For the purpose of this guidebook, we shall restrict ourselves to the tabla, which is the main percussion instrument for classical and semi-classical music. Although there are no rules dictating the rhythm cycles that are to be used for various sub-genres of raga sangeet, certain norms have become prevalent over the years which are followed for each.

CLASSICAL MUSIC RECITALS

The most commonly used *taals* for vocal khayal and khayal style instrumental recitals are the *teen taal* and *ek taal*, followed in popularity by the *roopak taal, jhap taal,* and *jhoomra taal.* There are, however, no binding rules in this regard and a composer/performer may choose any of these or any other *taal* for his *bandish.* The *teen taal* is also popular in kathak, in compositions where the emphasis is on footwork.

SEMI-CLASSICAL AND LIGHT-CLASSICAL MUSIC

These genres, which encompass thumri, dadra, and ghazal as well as instrumental and vocal accompaniments to kathak, make the most use of the *kehrwa, dadra,* and *roopak taal.* Qawwaali singing, which is a semi-classical sub-genre, also uses mostly *kehrwa taal,* traditionally on the dholak, sometimes backed up by the tabla.

TABLA SOLOS

The tabla, though a percussion instrument, remains a musical instrument none the less, capable of playing solos like all others. A tabla solo is called a *lehra* and is a unique development of the twentieth century, before which it was not common in public performances. It can be a riveting experience, either on stage or in a recording, to listen to a tabla lehra lasting up to half an hour or more. A tabaliya is said to come of age only when he can execute a lehra in one or two major taals. A tabla solo is usually accompanied by the harmonium, playing a soft, constant and repetitive lehra raga refrain, providing the tabaliya a melodic framework within which to 'fit' his *taal* patterns. A more sophisticated version of the tabla lehra uses the sarangi instead of the harmonium for accompaniment. Here again, mere verbalization may not be of much use compared to the actual, aural experience. A special mention is warranted of the noted tabaliya, Pandit Suresh Talwalkar. He has successfully experimented with a tabla solo being accompanied by a vocalist singing the accompanying refrain, whereas the reverse has been the practice since time immemorial. This is another instance of the open minded resilience of raga sangeet which does not bind musicians within needless restrictions and allows them the freedom to improvize, not only their music but also the methods of producing it. The only rules that cannot be broken are those of the musical purity of the ragas and faultless accuracy of the *taals*.

MAJOR TAAL CYCLES IN HINDUSTANI CLASSICAL MUSIC

A number of *taal* cycles have been mentioned at various places in the text of this book. We shall elaborate only on those *taals* which are in common, everyday use. Though already indicated, it may be reiterated that *taal* and *pakad* are two of the most distinguishing facets of a *bandish*. If a listener is able to identify the *taal* which is being played in a recital, and follow it from *sam* to *sam*, he is that much more able to enjoy raga sangeet to the fullest. There are a number of *Learn to play Tabla* books and CDs in the market which explain tabla rhythm cycles in detail. The bols and basic *thekas* of the more common *taals* are given below:

a. **Kehrwa taal:** This is the most rudimentary *taal* in Indian music, classical, semi-classical or folk. It has eight *matras* (beats) and is divided into two *khand-s* (chambers) of four *maatras* each, notated thus: 4-4. The first *maatra* of the first *khand* is a *taalee* and the first *maatra* of the second *khand* is a *khaalee*. The traditional bols of the *kehrwa* are: *Dha Gey Na Ti / Na Ka Dhi Na*. The *dha* in the first khand is a *taalee* and the *na* in the second khand , a *khaalee*. The correlation of *matras*, *khands*, *taalees*, *khaalees*, and their notation as shown for *kehrwa taal* above, has been used while describing the remaining *taal* cycles also.

b. **Daadra taal:** This is also a basic *taal*, much used in *thumris*, *daadras*, and ghazals. It has six *maatras* divided into two *khands* of three *maatras* each (3-3). The *taalee* is in the first *khand* and *khaalee* in the second. Its *bols* and *theka* are: *Dha Dhi Na / Dha Ti Na*.

c. **Teen taal:** Although a *taal* of pure classical pedigree, it is comparatively easy to follow due the simplicity of its *bols* and *khand* divisions. It is a sixteen beat *taal*, divided into four equal *khand-s* of four *maatras* each (4-4-4-4). The *taalee* is in the first, second, and fourth *khands*, while the *khaalee* is in the third *khand*. Because it has three *taalees*, it is called 'Teen (three) taal.' Its *theka* is as follows: *Dha Dhin Dhin Dha / Dha Dhin Dhin Dha / Dha Tin Tin Ta / Ta Dhin Dhin Dha*.The *sam*, as always, falls on the first *maatra* of this sixteen beat cycle, a rule which applies to all *taal* cycles as well. (In this case, the *sam* is on the first *dha* of the *theka* given above). *Teen taal* is not only the most popular *taal* among musicians but also lends itself beautifully to extensive improvization and audience participation, specially at the *sam*. Due to its familiarity with the public, it is most identifiable with Hindustani classical music.

d. **Ek taal:** A very commonly used *taal* in khayal, second only to the teen *taal* in popularity, it has twelve *maatras*, divided into six equal *khand*-s of two beats each (2-2-2-2-2-2). Its *theka* is as follows: *Dhin Dhin / Dhagey Tirkit / Tun Na / Kat Ta / Dhagey Tirkit / Dhin Na*. *Taalees* are in the first, third, fifth, and sixth *khand-s* while the *khaalees* fall in the second and fourth *khand*-s.

e. **Roopak taal**: A *taal* of seven beats but more complex due to the nature of its *bols* and *khand*-s. Its seven *maatras* are divided into three, *unequal khand*-s of 3-2-2 beats. Its *theka* is as follows: *Ti Ti Na / Dhi Na/ Dhi Na*. Its *taalees* are in the second and third *khand*-s, whereas *khaalee* is in the first *khand*. What gives *the roopak taal* its most dstinguishing feature is that it is the only *taal* where the *sam* falls on a *khaalee*. In all other *taals*, the *sam* falls on a *taalee*. *Roopak taal* is used in all types of classical and semi-classical music. It was a great favourite of the Ghazal Queen, Begum Akhtar.

f. **Jhap taal**: It is a *taal* of ten *maatras* divided into four *khand-s* of 2-3-2-3, the *taalees* being on the first, second and fourth *khand*-s and the *khaalee* in the third. Its *theka* is as follows: *Dhi Na / Dhi Dhi Na / Ti Na / Dhi Dhi Na*. This *taal* is also very popular and was much used in film songs in earlier days.

g. **Jhoomra taal**: This *taal* is comparatively rarely used but was a great favourite with the late maestro, Ustad Bade Ghulam Ali Khan. It has a swaying gait, as its name signifies, *Jhoom*, (meaning to sway.) It has fourteen *maatras* divided into four *khand*-s of 3-4-3-4. The *taal*ees fall in the first, second and fourth *khand-s*, with the *khaalee* in the third. Its *bols* and *theka* are as follows: *Dhin Dha Tirkit / Dhin Dhin Dhagey Tirkit / Tin Ta Tirkit / Dhin Dhin Dhagey Tirkit*. It is used exclusively in pure classical music and only by highly experienced musicians.

h. **Tihaayi**: As explained in an earlier chapter, a *tihaayi*, meaning triple, is an improvizatory rhythmic structure which is repeated three times, finally ending on the sam. It can have varying patterns, repeated thrice, invariably ending on the *sam* and is used in all the prevalent *taal*s of Hindustani classical music. It is basically an ornamental piece which can be resorted to by both, the main performer as well as the *tabaliya*. If the singer/instrumentalist carries on with the normal *bandish* while the percussionist executes a tri-cyclic rhythmic pattern; or if the *tabaliya* carries on with the normal *taal* while the vocalist repeats a melodic phrase three times, both are called a *tihaayi* and both will always ends on the *sam*. It is a very popular trick of the trade, easily identifiable even by a beginner and is used in folk and film music and kathak dance as well. It adds a most attractive ornamentation to any performance.

i   *Laggee*: A *laggee* is another ornamental structure created jointly by the main performer and the tabaliya, though executed primarily by the latter. It is used mainly in *thumri, daadra*, and ghazal. What it means is that while the vocalist continues singing the bandish, at a chosen point, the percussionist increases the tempo, first to double and then to quadruple speed. This point is generally reached when the performer has completed a stanza of poetry and is repeating it for a second or third time (for emphasis), the percussionist accelerates his tempo gradually, simultaneously improvising on the tabla bols as he first doubles and then quadruples the speed of the original *laya*. The *laggee* may last four, eight or more *taal* cycles but will invariably end on the sam, after which the percussionist reverts to the basic laya of the *bandish*. A two-fold increase in tempo is called a *Dugan,* a four-fold increase, a *Chaugan.* It is a highly ornamental technique which adds greatly to a vocal *thumri* or ghazal recital. It also forms the rhythmic basis for the spinning and swirling movements of the kathak dancer, reaching a crescendo that often concludes with a *tihaayi,* ending as always, on the *sam.* Only if a tabaliya is able to execute a really intricate and scintillating *laggee,* not a mere doubling or quadrupling of the tempo, is he considered a consummate percussionist. Ustad Bade Ghulam Ali Khan's favourite *tabaliya,* Ustad Nizamuddin Khan was a past master at the *laggee* and many of their best combinations are available on CDs and cassettes.

j. ***Aardha:*** *Aardha* means askew, oblique, or crooked. Among *tabla* techniques, it occupies a very prominent place and entails the percussionist deliberately going obliquely 'against the grain' of the *taal* to which the *bandish* is set. This is clearly discernible when one hears it, though it is that much more difficult to explain in words. If he is playing the *teentaal* of sixteen beats, the percussionist will execute an *aardha* in such a way that that though the *laya* remains same and the cycle also takes the same time to go round, yet the time lag between beats is so expertly and unevenly varied so as to give it a skewed, crooked feel. An *aardha* may go on for a few *taal* cycles before reverting to normal. It is a highly ornamental variation; this time, a spontaneous *upaj* by the tabaliya.

k. **Other Ornamental techniques**: The percussionist has a bagful of tricks up his sleeve to enliven and illuminate a recital. Some of these are *Paran, Mohra, Peshkaar, Qaaida,* and *Relaa,* basically all decorative techniques, varying the tempo of an ongoing *bandish*, providing variety and *upaj*, before returning to the original *theka*. These could be considered ornamentations or *alankaars* of the tabla. Ornamentation and grace are fundamental and integral to Hindustani classical music, of which the tabla is an inseparable part.

FAMOUS TABALIYAS, PAST AND PRESENT

After Pandit Ravi Shankar and Ustad Ali Akbar Khan raised the artistic prestige of the percussionist by their personal example, the tabaliya began making a place for himself in the hierarchy of musicians. Before that, he was an unknown entity beating time to the main performer, his presence barely acknowledged and his name never mentioned in any brochure, leaflet or record cover. Though a few artistes like Ustad Karamatullah Khan, Pandits Kishan Maharaj, Shamta Prasad and Chatur Lal as also Ustad Ahmed Jaan *Thirakwa* were well known for their tremendous solos and their performances as accompanists, it was only after the intervention of the sitar-sarod duo mentioned above that the lot of the tabaliyas, in general, rose in respectability and their names began gaining mention on record labels and concert brochures. Apart from the above mentioned, the great tabaliyas of the last fifty years include Ustad Allah Rakha and Pandit Kanai Dutta.Current leading lights of the tabla include Ustads Zakir Hussain and Taufiq Qureshi, sons of Ustad Allah Rakha and Ustad Sabir Khan, son of Ustad Karamatullah, Pandit Bickram Ghosh, son of Pandit Shankar Ghosh, Pandits Swapan Choudhuri, Anand Gopal Mukhopadhyay, Shubhankar Bannerji, Kumar Bose, Sanjay Chatterjee, and Sudhir Pande, to mention a few.

RHYTHM CYCLES: TAAL PATTERNS AND UNIQUE QUALITIES OF THE TABLA

Even at the risk of repetition, it bears reiteration that rhythm plays such a vital role in Hindustani classical music that without it, the genre would be reduced to a skeleton, devoid of its life-blood. Accordingly, some random thoughts are mentioned below to highlight the centrality of the tabla in raga sangeet.

While *swar* remains preeminent as a whole, when it comes to *bandish* compositions, the two other ingredients of raga sangeet, viz, *taal* and *laya* also come into full play. The *taal* to which a *bandish* has been set is a cardinal constituent of a Hindustani classical music recital. It provides the rhythmic spine to the melody and the musician's improvizations thereon. Its constant regularity and faultless accuracy lay down the 'boundary posts' within which the performer's flights of imagination, however fanciful, have to confine themselves.

The percussionist, while sustaining the poetic metre of the lyrics also enhances the melodic beauty of the *bandish* by providing a worthy counterpoise to it, thus elevating the overall appeal of a recital. After all, music is a performing art and enhancing listeners' aesthetic enjoyment is the endeavour of every performer. The growing trend of concert hall recitals as well as recording studios is now towards recitals of limited duration. This demands that recitals be made as interesting as possible within their reduced duration.

With a view to providing an 'attractive package,' music company managers tend to introduce the spectacular or sensational percussionist in the hope that this will enhance audience participation. This is not a welcome development and is frowned upon by musicologists. They view it as an undesirable factor that mars the aesthetic appeal of *swar* and *laya* and lays an unhealthy over-emphasis on the percussionist's dramatics and speed at the cost of the overall *ras-bhava* of a recital.[6]

A series of albums featuring Ustad Allah Rakha and his sons, Zakir Hussain and Taufiq Qureshi retain their lasting popularity and there are many other new *tabaliyas* who have come out with solos. This has been a very welcome development. Earlier, this instrument was never given its due as a result of which the status of the *tabalchi* remained that of a second class artiste for many years. Being the very base upon which a musical composition stands, this inequality needed to be corrected. This correction was applied by Ustad Ali Akbar Khan and Pandit Ravi Shankar in the 1950-60s, by according equal status to their percussionists with the happy result that the latter often achieved fame and fortune to match their mentors'.

The centrality of *taal* and its correlation with *swar* and *laya* have been explained above. In order to enjoy any kind of music, it is essential that we are familiar with the rhythm cycle which the music is set to. Indian folk music is set to rudimentary *taal* cylcles. Hindi film songs too generally use just two or three basic *taal*s. This was not always so and from the 1950s to the mid-1980s (called the Golden Age of Hindi cinema) many film music directors infused a good deal of raga sangeet into their music. It was quite common to hear songs which were not only raga-based but were also set to the more intricate *taal*s generally associated with classical music.

Film songs with a classical base were very popular among the public in those days. Among the last films to have music of this quality was Shyam Benagal's *Sardari Begum* and Muzaffar Ali's *Umrao Jaan*. The disappearance of the raga-based element from films today can be attributed to the poor quality of music directors as well as the falling tastes of movie audiences. Both have contributed to the alienation of younger generations from classical music. It is worth mentioning the contributions of some great vocalists to old film classics: Ustad Amir Khan and Pandit D.V. Paluskar sang for the film *Baiju Bawra* in 1955, as did Ustad Bade Ghulam Ali Khan for the magnum opus, *Mughal-e-Azam*. Mohammad Rafi's classical *bandish* in Raga *Hameer*, '*Madhuban mein Raadhika naachey rey, Girdhar ki muraliya baajey rey*' for the film *Kohinoor* (1960) remains a perennial favourite and is regularly featured on TV.

15

Semi-classical Music: The Fabulous World of Thumri and Kathak

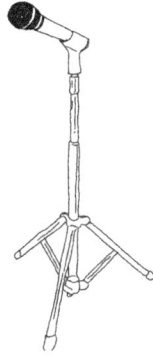

HISTORICAL BACKGROUND

The word *thumri* comprises *thumak,* the coquettish, sideways throw of the hip by a (female) dancer and *ree,* belonging to, or associated with. *Thumri* is thus a genre associated with coquetry and merriment. After the first quarter of the 18th century, *dhrupad* had begun to decay into a dry and technical art, devoid of the element of joy. Just as the danger of extinction always brings with it the hope of rejuvenation, *dhrupad* yielded, in part, to the khayal which rejuvenated Hindustani classical music and both styles continued as the principal singing styles till the end of the 19th century. With the advent of the Europeans and the East India Company during the nineteenth century, a further loosening up of existing norms resulted in musicians vying with each other to retain their patrons' favour by experimenting with even lighter forms of music.

Thus was born the *thumri.* Although it became very popular and remains even today one of the most beautiful genres of raga sangeet, it grew mainly as a semi-classical genre which neither sought to replace the khayal nor did people accept it as such. Today, even the 'greatest of the greats,' whose names are synonymous with khayal gayaki, are also known for their *thumris.* Geniuses like the sitar virtuoso, Ustad Vilayat Khan have played some of the most exquisite *thumris* ever conceived. Ustads Nazaakat and Salaamat Ali recorded their immortal *jugalbandi* in the *Pahadi thumri, Saiyyan bina ghar soona*, which remains unparalleled to this day. *Laggee* plays a major part of percussion accompaniment in *thumri* and kathak dance, as explained in the previous chapter. In the Nazaakt-Salaamat *thumri* mentioned above, Ustad Allah Rakha's *lagee* is so flambuoyant and mesmerizing that I do not think the world will ever hear the likes of it again.

Other singers have acquired name and fame solely on the merit of their *thumri* singing, such as Begum Akhtar, Girija Devi, Rasoolan Bai, Naina Devi, Badi Moti Bai, Shanti Hiranand and Siddhheshwari Devi. Among the present generation, musicians who have attained great heights in *thumri* singing/playing alongside their other achievements, are Pandit Ajoy Chakraborty, Ustad Rashid Khan (both vocal) and Ustad Shahid Parvez (sitar) and Pandit Hari Prasad Chaurasia, to name just a few. A mistaken belief exists that there are two styles, or *ang-s*, of *thumri* singing, viz, the Poorbi (Eastern) *ang* and the Punjabi *ang*, which is a fallacy. Musicologists are clear that there is only one thumri style and that is the *poorbi ang*. Traditionally, the home of the *poorbi thumri* is the Lucknow-Benaras-Gaya belt. This mistaken belief has come about due to the fact that some singers from Punjab, notably those of the Patiala and Sham Chaurasi (Hoshiarpur) gharanas, had achieved such fame and fortune with their elaborate and scintillating *thumris* that listeners began referring to their singing style as the Punjabi *ang* of *thumri*.

The traditional poorbi ang *thumri* described above is essentially *deshi* or rustic in character due to its lyrics which are couched in the Poorbiya dialect. This dialect is meticulously maintained even when they are sung by singers adept in chaste Urdu. Many of the stylistic nuances of *thumri* and ghazal gayaki are common, even though the former is thoroughly rustic in character and the latter excessively courtly. These nuances are the repetitions of lyrics, particularly in the antara and use of *laggee* during these repetitions, culminating in *tihayis* ending on the *sam*. *Laggee* and *sam* have been explained in detail in the chapter devoted to rhythm cycles in percussion. Scholar-musicians often do not accord *thumri* its due, nor do their Lec-dems or those organized by Spic-Macay include much of it in their curriculum. This is a serious shortcoming. *Thumri* is the most natural calling of any Indian with a musical ear and must come first and foremost in his quest to becoming an informed listener or *rasik*.

BASIC QUALITIES OF THUMRI

Although a semi-classical vein, *thumri* retains all the musical purity of Hindustani classical music, i.e. the emphasis on *swar, taal,* and *laya*. The 'lighter vein' is lent to it, among other factors, by its choice of ragas. Great composers have conceived thumri *bandishes* based on ragas (often belonging to the Deshi stream such as *pahari, peeloo,* and *maand* etc) which have a lighter temperament and are better suited to *thumri* in their mood-emotional content (*ras-bhava*.) The distinctive accent on the *pakad* of the raga, retains its overarching importace in *thumri* as well. In short, there is no dilution of the rules in *thumri* singing vis-à-vis khayal. The second quality of the *thumri* lies in its shorter duration as compared to the khayal. Within this reduced time frame, the performer has to display his or her forte in *gat-*

kaari, taan-kaari and *laya-kaari,* bring out the *pakad* clearly, while evoking the full *ras-bhava* of the raga. Musicians like Ustad Bade Ghulam Ali Khan, who was nonpareil in this genre, have raised the *thumri* to such heights of classical brilliance as to eclipse even their own khayal gayaki in the process. Begum Akhtar, on the other hand, did not sing khayals at all, yet raised her thumri singing to such classical heights as to match any khayal gayak.

In the *thumri,* the elaborate *alap* is done away with and the performer has to make do with a short *aochaar,* if at all. A third quality, also the USP of *thumri* is its intense romanticism and *joie de vivre* or exuberant celebration of life. That is why ragas of a lighter temperament are chosen for *thumri bandishes.* Lastly, the aspect that lends it an aura of lightness, romance and merriment is that all *thumri bandishes* are set to the simpler rhythm cycles like *kehrwa* and *daadra taals.* This aspect also endears the *thumri* to kathak dance as an accompaniment. All the elements of the mental chemistry between musician and *rasik* such as *aankhen chaar karnaa* come alive in a *thumri,* raising the emotive content of a recital to sensuous dimensions. This is particularly so where the lyrical theme of a *bandish* is *virah* or *viyog,* the separated lover's lament.

Such is the magic of *thumri* that some famous Hindi film music directors in the 1960s and '70s built their careers composing one hit song after another, based on the *thumri bandishes* of old masters like Barkat Ali Khan, younger brother of Ustad Bade Ghulam Ali Khan. So powerful is the emotional pull of the *thumri* that even instrumentalists have made it a regular part of their repertoire. The wordless *thumris* of Ustad Vilayat Khan and Pandit Hari Prasad Chaurasia on the *sitar* and flute, respectively (both coincidentally in raga *Pahaadi*) are as alluring in their romantic appeal as any *thumri* sung by a vocalist, replete with the most beautiful lyrical poetry. Both these instrumental *thumris* are included in the 'short duration *bandish*' album *Romantic Pahaadi* mentioned in the chapter entitled 'Recommended Progress: In Stages and by Genres'. This semi-classical genre of raga sangeet is collectively also called *thumri-daadra*.

GHAZALS

A ghazal is a literary composition and not a musical one. It is a collection of couplets of two lines each. Such a couplet is called a *Sh'er*. The first couplet of the ghazal is called the *Matla* (rising) in which both lines rhyme with each other. In all the other *sh'er*-s, only the second lines rhyme with the *matla*. Each *sh'er* stands by itself as an independent thought and is not connected to the others. The concluding *sh'er* is called the *Maqt'a* which often contains the nom de plume or *takhallus* of the poet (*Shair*.) Every song composed in Urdu is, therefore, not a ghazal, which must follow the rules for rhyme, metre and content explained above. Other forms of Urdu poetry are Nazm, Rubaiyyat and Geet, etc. Ghazal singing is being included in this book solely for the reason that many high class *ghazal* singers sing in the semi-classical *'thumri* style', complete with all the artistic embellishments explained in the preceding paragraphs. This style was personified by Begum Akhtar and flourished in Awadh. Even though *thumri*-style ghazal singers have been few and far between, their influence has been so marked and their reach so wide that their contributions have engendered an entirely new sub-genre of semi-classical music. In a few instances, their singing won such critical acclaim that they were welcomed into the classical fraternity with alacrity.

To site an instance, when the famous sarodiya, Ustad Amjad Ali Khan gave his major concert as a young man in the 1960s, the one person whose appreciation he sought most and valued above all others was Begum Akhtar, the renowned ghazal and *thumri* singer of Lucknow (d.1974). She was known for her mastery over *swar, taal,* and *laya* which earned her such widespread respect among the pundits of raga sangeet that she remains unequalled in the art of ghazal and *thumri* gayaki to this day. The touchstone of the traditional ghazal is that it readily lends itself as vocal accompaniment to kathak dance, as exemplified in the ghazals which Asha Bhosle sang under the music direction of Khayyam for Muzaffar Ali's classic film, *Umrao Jaan* and which accompanied the kathak dances performed by actress Rekha.

Not many ghazal singers sing in the *thumri* style. In fact, only a miniscule minority do. The majority choose the filmy *geet* style. That way, they are able to attract a wider audience, one that may neither be familiar with Urdu poetry nor have an ear for *thumri*. Among this majority, the name of Jagjit Singh (d. 2011) comes on top. A classically trained singer-composer with a highly sonorous voice that charmed millions for over three decades, Jagjit Singh consciously chose *not* to sing in the *thumri* style. By far the most talented singer of non-classical music in India, he brought into full play his individual forte which was replete with classical ornamentations like *meend, gamak* and *taan,* yet managed to keep his ghazals clearly outside the *thumri* mould and firmly within the *'geet'* style. He did this by setting his ghazals to catchy, filmy rhythms, using western instruments like the guitar, violin, and saxophone.

Nevertheless, for the beginner, Jagjit Singh is an excellent starting point for vocal music, as he exemplifies all the finest ornamental nuances (*alankaar*) of raga-based gayaki, even though his ghazals are not set in the *thumri* format, for reasons stated above. Another ghazal singer of immense potential is Hariharan. Originally a Carnatic prodigy, he first made a successful foray into ghazal gayaki in the '80s and '90s, followed by a sensational entry into Indi-pop along with Leslie Lewis as *The Colonial Cousins*. By his own admission, ghazal singing places maximum demands on his expertise as he has to remain faithful to the tenets of Hindustani classical music on the one hand, while imparting the poet's emotions to the ghazal he is singing, on the other. Moreover, the words and phrases have to be emphasized in perfect consonance with *swar*, *laya* and *taal*. A ghazal singer of great renown in the semi-classical, raga-based *thumri* style is Ghulam Ali of Pakistan. He has been around for a long time and will also give the beginner a head start in his quest. A suggestion for those not conversant with Urdu: they could disregard (not discard) the poetry and concentrate on the music, even though aficionados may consider such a suggestion sacrilegious.

KATHAK

Kathak is one of the eight forms of Indian classical dance. It traces its origins to the ancient nomadic bards of northern India called kathak-s or storytellers. These bards performed in village squares and temple courtyards, recounting mythological and moral tales from the scriptures, embellishing their recitals with hand gestures and facial expressions along with instrumental and vocal music. From the sixteenth century onwards, it absorbed certain additional features from Persian and Central Asian dance which were imported by the Mughals. There are three major gharanas of kathak from which performers draw their lineage: the gharanas of Jaipur, Lucknow and Varanasi/Benaras (originating in the courts of the Rajput kings of Jaipur/Amber; the Nawab of Oudh/ Lucknow, and the temples of Varanasi, respectively). There is also a less prominent (and later) Raigarh gharana which amalgamated techniques from all the three preceding it, but became famous for its own distinctive compositions as well.

The name Kathak is derived from the Sanskrit *kathaa* meaning story, and *kathaakaar* meaning one who tells a story. Properly, it is pronounced *kathhak* with a double emphasis on the middle consonant. Today, however, the simpler kathak is acceptable. *'Kathaa kahey so kathak'* is a popular saying which translates as 'one who tells a story, is a kathak' or 'that which tells a story, is kathak.' The structure of a conventional kathak performance follows a progression in tempo from slow to fast, ending with a dramatic climax. A short composition is known as a *tukra,* a longer one as a *toda.* There are also compositions consisting solely of footwork. The performer often engages in rhythmic play with the *taal* cycle, splitting it into triplets or quintuplets for example, which is marked out in the footwork as a counterpoint to the rhythm of the percussion. From the above, it is evident that kathak is closely associated with Hindustani classical music in every respect, particularly rhythm cylces and *laya* patterns.

ABHINAYA AND KATHAK COMPOSITIONS

All compositions are performed so that the final step of the dancer and beat of the percussion, lands exactly on the *sam* i.e. first beat of the *taal* cycle. Most compositions also have *bols* (rhythmic words) which serve as mnemonics to the composition. This recitation of bols is known as *padhant* and is aurally very interesting when presented this way. The *bols* may be borrowed from the *tabla* (e.g. *dha, ge, na, tirkit*) or be taken from the a dancer's movements itself (*ta, thei, tat, ta ta, tigda, digdig*). Often *tukras* are composed to highlight specific aspects of the dance, for example the *chakkarwaala tukra* which showcases the signature *chakkars* or spins of kathak. The spin is generally executed on the heel, manifesting itself towards the end of the *tukra*, often repeatedly. Five, nine, fifteen, or more sequential spins are common. These *tukras* are popular with audiences as they are visually exciting and are executed at great speed.

Abhinaya means acting or expressing emotions. Apart from the traditional *abhinaya* pieces performed to a bhajan, ghazal or *thumri*, kathak also has a style of expression called *bhaav bataanaa* (literally, to show emotion). It is a mode where *abhinaya* dominates, and arose in Mughal times. It is more suited to the *mehfil* or the *darbaar* style of royal court environment. Because of the close proximity of the performer to the courtly audience, the latter can more easily see the nuances of the dancer's facial expressions. Consequently, it translates to a concert stage recital with some difficulty. First, a *thumri* is sung and once the mood is set, a line from the *thumri* is interpreted with facial *abhinaya* and hand movements. This can continue for an indefinite period, limited only by the dancer's interpretative abilities.

DEVELOPMENTS DURING THE MEDEIVAL, MUGHAL AND BRITISH PERIODS

By the thirteenth century, a definite style had emerged and soon technical features like mnemonic syllables came into usage.

Later, the advent of the Bhakti movement brought with it the emergence of *raas-leela*, based on the legend of Lord Krishna, Radha, and the Gopis. It narrated tales from their lives and included Krishna's exploits in Vrindaavan and tales from his childhood, called *Krishna-leela* and *Baal-leela* respectively. The dance also began to be influenced by folk elements of the common people, through whom it reached the Mughal court. Here it encountered different forms of dance and music, most especially those imported from Persia. Dancers were enticed from the temples to the courts by gifts and royal favour. Patronage soared as a social class of dancers and courtiers emerged in the royal palaces. The environment of the Mughal courts caused a shift in focus of kathak from a purely religious, bhakti art form to that of courtly, *darbaari* entertainment. Dancers from the Middle East spread their ideas among kathak dancers and in turn, borrowed from kathak to enrich their own. Kathak absorbed new ideas and adapted them in its own vocabulary. This synthesis was similar to the confluence that occurred between the indigenous, *shastric* music of pre-tenth-eleventh century India, and the incoming Persian and Central Asian traditions thereafter, leading to the development of a composite whole. Elements of *tarana* gayaki are also evident in the *bol*s of vocal music that accompanies this dance form.

Kathak also began to shift away from other traditional Indian dances such as the Bharatanatyam and evolved its own, individual identity. The *demi-plié* (bent at the knees) stance of most other Indian dances gave way to straight legged stance taken from Persian dancers. To highlight the elaborate rhythmic footwork, ankle bells or *ghungroos* were tied on the legs from the ankles to just below the knees. It was during this period that the signature spins mentioned above, were introduced, possibly influenced by the 'whirling dervishes' of the Sufi traditions of Mevlana Shamsuddin 'Tabrizi' and his disciple, Jalaaluddin 'Rumi'. The straight-legged position gave a new vitality to the footwork, which wove percussive rhythms in its own right, together with the rhythms of the tabla or *pakhawaj*. Besides percussion, kathak is also accompanied by the sitar, flute or *Dilruba* (also called *Esraaj*, which is a *sarangi* lookalike bowed instument but with frets like the sitar.) Although now it is substantially different from other Indian dance forms, kathak retains its ancient ties and still displays consanguinity with the others, particularly in the hand-formations and stances such as the *Tribhangi* posture (triangular stance, as seen in pictures of Krishna playing the flute) which is common to most Indian dances.

Many factors contributed to the growth and development of kathak. Nawab Wajid Ali Shah of Oudh (Awadh) not only extended patronage to kathak but also danced himself under the tutelage of Durga Prasad, an ancestor of Pandit Birju Maharaj. The Nawab thus aided the expansion of technical vocabulary of kathak, which forms the basis of its most influential Lucknow gharana. The Lakhnavi style emphasizes subtlety of expression and grace of movement, called *nazaakat*. The Nawab continued his patronage of kathak even after his dethronement and exile to Calcutta in 1856 and upto his death there thirty years later. The Lucknow style contrasts sharply with the Jaipur school, which is renowned for its flamboyant footwork. The *Kotha* tradition, performed by professional dancing girls *(tawaaif)* succeeded the *darbaari* style after the dissolution of princely states and their courts. It differs from the latter, involving more

Nakhraa (mischievous flirtation with its clientele.) As the dance teachers at the *kothas* were also often teachers at the courts, a free interchange of ideas took place between the two milieus, helping to broaden and consolidate the repertoire of kathak.

KATHAK TODAY

Kathak has fully regained its popularity and dignity and is now acknowledged as one of the classical dances of India. Its current form is a synthesis of all the inputs of the past, where its courtly and romantic aspects sit comfortably alongside the mythological and the religious. The descendants of Binda Deen, Kalka Prasad and Shambhu Maharaj, now called the Maharaj family, have contributed immensely to this tradition. The gharana is now headed by Pandit Birju Maharaj, the greatest kathak dancer alive today. It will be a grave injustice if he is not honoured with the Bharat Ratna, which has already been awarded to the Carnatic vocalist M.S. Subhalaksmi, Pandits Ravi Shankar and Bhimsen Joshi and Lata Mangeshkar. His disciple, Saswati Sen also performed in Satyajit Ray's movie masterpiece, *Shatranj ke Khilari* in which Birjuji also sang a thumri. Another renowned dancer, Sitara Devi, daughter of Sukhdev Maharaj and disciple of Acchan Maharaj of Benaras, has been one of its leading lights since the mid-twentieth century. Her lively, zestful, and fiery performances will ever remain a benchmark for generations to come. The magnificent art of complex and scintillating footwork of the Jaipur gharana is being kept alive by the Gangani family, earlier Sunderlal, and now Rajendra Gangani.

16

Recommended Progress in Stages and by Genres

GENERAL GUIDELINES

Three aspects have been kept in mind while formulating this list. Firstly, comfort level. As mentioned earlier, vocal music can be rough on the uninitiated ear as compared to its instrumental variant. Secondly, ease of comprehension. Hindustani classical music, being a unique cultural experience, needs to be explored step by step, from the simpler genres to the more elaborate ones. This entails listening in the early stages to music that is more basic in content in terms of melody and rhythm and gradually progressing to the more complex. Lastly, the thumb rule of 'instrumental first and vocal next.' The beginner's journey should progress in the following stages:-

Stage 1: (Semi-classical and light music genres; *thumri, daadra,* ghazals, and 'Lounge music.') The best help to the beginner in this regard could come from young *rasiks*, sales staff at large music malls like Planet M and from shop owners of small stores, particularly the latter. The best listeners (and sellers) of good Hindustani music (classical as well as semi-classical) are to be found in Mumbai, Pune, and Kolkata. Delhi as well as UP (Lucknow and Benaras) also have their share of *rasiks* though the last mentioned, once their very home, has lately fallen on lean times. The most attractive features of *thumri* and ghazal have already been enumerated in the chapter on that subject. Accordingly, in stage-1, *thumris* and *daadras* are recommended. Recently, old *thumri* recordings of Ustads Nazaakat Ali and Salaamat Ali have also been re-released into the market, which are an excellent starting point for beginners. We can now add Lounge music to this category as well. With a view to gaining access to larger audiences (made up in major part by keen but classically uninitiated listeners), lounge music makes liberal use of electronics and the latest recording techniques. Some highly commendable music has been created by Abhijeet Pohankar, a musician with a classical lineage. *Piya Basanti Re* by Ustad Sultan Khan (vocals and *sarangi*) is an excellent example of this new genre. The Wadali brothers (Padmashris Puranchand and Pyarelal) who have recently broken on the scene have been singing *naatiya kalaam* (a form of sufi folk) on radio and national TV for many years. They have been introduced into lounge music by Times Music with their latest album *Yaad Piya ki*. The eponymous title song of this album is an old and well loved thumri of Ustad Bade Ghulam Ali Khan and an excellent piece on its own, bringing out the full potential of the Wadalis' highly melodious and powerful voices, against a backdrop of haunting electronic music. Purbayan Chatterji and his Shastriya Syndicate have already been mentioned in the section related to lounge music. Newer albums are coming out every day which listeners can seek out for themselves. However, it must be remembered that the beginner is listening to lounge music as a prelude to graduating to higher levels of Hindustani classical music. The prelude is not an end in itself. Above all, lounge music should be listened to as a genre by itself and not be confused with fusion music, the latter being an exercise in futility.

Stage 2: (Instrumental Classical music) The CD/MP3 revolution of the twenty-first century has brought in its wake sales promotion schemes of questionable ethics. Unsold stocks are repackaged and sold as music 'for healing', 'for meditation,' 'for yoga', etc. Any sales pitch that touts music as being for anything other than for listening is a gimmick. (The shehnai played during traditional Indian weddings is the only exception to this rule.) Incidentally, the shehnai was never a classical instrument in the first place. It waited for hundreds of years for Ustad Bismillah Khan to single handedly elevate it to that level. Now there are many shehnai *vaadaks* playing excellent raga sangeet, Ustad Ali Ahmed Hussein being the best at present. The instruments which are most soothing and easiest on the ear are the santoor, flute, sitar, sarod, and shehnai. Among their best known exponents are Pandits Shiv Kumar Sharma (santoor), Hari Prasad Chaurasia (flute), Ustad Ali Akbar Khan (sarod), and Ustad Bismillah Khan (shehnai) respectively. The sarangi, the 'instrument with the human voice' has, unfortunately, not produced many recording artistes with the exception of Pandit Ram Narayan, an old stalwart of great standing and Ustad Sultan Khan, a great classicist who made a name in lounge music as well, a few years before his sad demise in 2011. There are innumerable other exponents, past and present, playing these instruments and their recordings are available widely. These are Ustad Shahid Parvez and Pandit Budhaditya Mukherjee (sitar), Pandit Ronu Majumdar (flute) and Pandits Tarun Bhattacharya and Bhajan Sopori (both santoor). Solo tabla recitals have a charm of their own, especially for those with an ear for rhythm. Other instruments used in raga sangeet are the Hawaiian guitar (Pandit Vishva Mohan Bhatt), the violin (Pandit V.G. Jog and Vidushi N. Rajam) and the *surbahar*, a larger, more sonorous version of the sitar (Ustad Imrat Khan.) Recently, the Mandolin and the Spanish guitar have also joined the fraternity, though they are yet to prove their mettle in the Hindustani classical arena.

Stage 3: (Classical vocal genre; khayal singing) As maintained throughout this guidebook, vocal music is the bedrock of raga sangeet. Hence it comes last on the ladder and requires that much more effort to enjoy, appreciate and understand. Within the gharanas of pure classical vocalists too, a graduated progression of three sub-stages has been worked out, which the beginner may follow in order to remain within the general guidelines enumerated above. However, since gharanas are slowly becoming obsolescent by merging with one another, it is better to spell out this progression by naming the individual singers directly, whose recordings beginners could listen to. This graduated progression is not an indication of the superiority of one gharana over another but is based solely on the ease of assimilation by the newly initiated *rasik*, in order to make his entry into vocal music a smooth and enjoyable one. The three sub-stages are enumerated in the succeeding paragraphs.

In the first sub-stage, the foremost name is that of Ustad Bade Ghulam Ali Khan. He is followed by his artistic successor, Pandit Ajoy Chakraborty, even though the latter was never personally tutored by the former but by his son, Ustad Munawwar Ali Khan. All three belong to the Patiala tradition. The Patiala gharana style of singing is the easiest on the uninitiated ear. Closely affiliated to the Patiala style is the gayaki of Ustads Nazaakat Ali and Salaamat Ali Khan of the Sham Chaurasi gharana. Their music is exquisitely sweet and easy on the ear. (It may be noted that these singers feature in both stages, i.e. stages 1 and 3. This is because they are *chaumukhi* gayaks who have sung *thumris* as well as khayals with equal aplomb.)

In the second sub-stage of this vocal-classical progression is Ustad Amir Khan. He is by far the most 'complete' Hindustani classical musician to feature in the entire canon since the advent of recorded music. Although primarily associated with the Indore gharana and subsequently with Bhendi Bazaar (Bombay), he was actually a class by himself. During his prime, he evolved his own style that encompassed all that is the very best and most pristine in the Hindustani Classical tradition, shedding some of the excess baggage of *gharaanedar* gayaki. His immense intellect led him to examine a raga through the microscope of a scientist and identify its essential character. Thereafter, he carefully organized his performances and recordings in such a manner as to bring out the full spectrum of each raga in all its many-splendoured colours. Beginners are advised to listen to Ustad Amir Khan as much as they can and acquire at least one album of his. Like owning a Rolls-Royce, it is a possession for life. Ustad Amir Khan thus stands out as the ideal 'link' between the gentleness of the Patiala/Sham Chaurasi stable and the more tempestuous styles of the third sub-stage, which is the last step in our vocal progression.

This sub-stage is associated with the gharanas of Kiraana, Jaipur-Atrauli, Rampur-Sehswaan, Benaras and Agra, in the 'ascending order of tempestuousness', if one may use the phrase. The most prominent singers, past and present, associated with these gharanas are Pandit Bhimsen Joshi (Kiraana), Vidushi Kishori Amonkar and Pandit Mallikarjun Mansur (both Jaipur-Atrauli gharana), Ustads Nissar Hussain and Ghulam Mustafa Khan (both Rampur), Pandits Rajan and Sajan Mishra (jugalbandi brothers of Benaras), and Ustad Faiyyaz Khan (Agra) respectively. Others who form part of this third sub-stage are Ustad Vilayat Hussain Khan, Ustad Lataafat Hussain Khan, Pandit Omkaar Nath Thakur, and Ustad Rashid Khan.

To summarize Stage 3, the beginner is advised to enter the field of khayal gayaki starting with Ustad Bade Ghulam Ali Khan, Pandit Ajoy Chakraborty and the brothers Nazaakat Ali-Salaamat Ali. Thereafter, using the meticulously organized recordings of the Indore doyen, Ustad Amir Khan as a link, he should enter the third and final stage of the remaining gharanas of Kiraana, Jaipur-Atrauli, Rampur-Sehswan, Benaras, and Agra. Modern masters like Ustad Rashid Khan, though brought up in the Rampur style (by his guru, Ustad Nissar Hussein at the ITC Sangeet Research Academy, Kolkata) are gradually evolving into composite singers, perfecting their individual forte by adopting the best from other traditions. This is as it should be. In other words, most of the top class, younger vocalists of today sing in a composite style, incorporating what they feel is the best from various gharanas preceding them. It only adds to their charm if they retain some of the finer aspects of the gharanas bequeathed to them by their gurus. The choice is wide and varied once we enter the last stage of vocal Hindustani classical music.

Recommended Listening: Music Albums Listed in Progressive Stages

We have discussed the progressive stages through which a beginner's listening should progress as he makes his way into the world of Hindustani classical music. Given below are details of music albums, *listed in the same progressive stages*, which beginners are advised to listen to. Listeners can also visit websites such as www.saregama.com, www.t-series.com,

and www.inrecohindusthan.com and devise their own list, in
the recommended progression given below.

Stage 1: (Semi-classical music: Light instrumental, *Thumri/
Daadra* and Ghazals)
- 'Call of the Valley': Pandits Shiv Kumar Sharma and Hari
  Prasad Chaurasia (flute and santoor).
- Jagjit Singh (ghazals) All recordings.
- Ghulam Ali (ghazals) All recordings.
- Begum Akhtar (ghazals, *thumris, and daadras*) All recordings.
- Hariharan (ghazals)
- *Thumri: The Music of Love*: Ustad Bade Ghulam Ali Khan
  (RPG Saregama, CDNF 150250 ADD)* Immortal *thumris*.
- *Golden Milestones*: Ustads Nazaakat Ali & Salaamat Ali Khan,
  (RPG Saregama, CDNF 150528)* A rare masterpiece.
- *Yaad Piya Ki*: Wadali Brothers (Times Music, TDIGH 048V)

Stage 2: (Instrumental Classical) Khayal-based recitals by
the following artistes:-
- Ustad Vilayat Khan (sitar)
- Pandit Nikhil Bannerji (sitar)
- Pandit Hari Prasad Chaurasia (flute)
- Pandit Shiv Kumar Sharma (santoor)
- Ustad Bismillah Khan (shehnai)
- Ustad Ali Ahmed Hussein (shehnai)
- Pandit Ram Narain (sarangi)
- Ustad Sabri Khan (sarangi)
- Ustad Sultaan Khan (sarangi)
- Ustad Ali Akbar Khan (sarod)
- Ustad Amjad Ali Khan (sarod)
- Pandit Vishwa Mohan Bhatt (Hawaiian guitar/*mohan veena*)

Stage 3: (Vocal Classical)

- Ustad Bade Ghulam Ali Khan (RPG Saregama, CDNF 150193 ADD). Eleven short *drut* khayal *bandish*es of three to five minutes each. A unique collection.
- Ustad Bade Ghulam Ali Khan (RPG Saregama, CDNF 150145 AAD). Full length Khayals in ragas *Gunkali* and *Maalkauns*.
- Ustads Nazaakat Ali and Salaamat Ali Khan: *Golden Milestones* (RPG Saregama, CDNF 150528).
- Ustad Amir Khan.
- Pandit Bhimsen Joshi.
- Vidushi Kishori Amonkar.
- Ustad Nissar Hussain Khan.
- Ustad Vilayat Hussain Khan.
- Ustad Faiyyaz Khan *Collections from Hindustan Records* (Hindusthan, IP-6003 AAD)* An old masterpiece.

17

Historical Significance of Bengal in the 19th and 20th Centuries

Neither does Bengal feature in the evolution of Hindustani classical music in ancient or medieval times nor is any of the original gharanas of music associated with it. Yet, from the mid-19th century onwards, almost half of all the action in this field was taking place in Calcutta (the rest was happening in Bombay and Lahore). Calcutta's sphere of influence grew even larger as the century ran out and the Indian cinema and recording industries came into being in the early 20th century. There were a number of historical events that occurred, as a result of which this extraordinary state of affairs came to pass.

ANNEXATION OF AWADH BY THE EAST INDIA COMPANY AND EXILE OF THE NAWAB

Awadh (colonial Oudh), the geographical area around present day Lucknow, Kanpur, and Allahabad, was a prosperous kingdom and a great centre of the arts, most notably Hindustani music, Urdu and Persian poetry and kathak dance, not to speak of its exquisite cuisine, embroidery, and perfumery. By an earlier treaty, the East India Company had granted it a special status as a separate kingdom, independent of the Mughals. By 1856, however, the Governor General of

India, Lord Dalhousie, concluded that Oudh was being very badly governed by its 'debauched' king, Nawab Wajid Ali Shah and unilaterally decided to abrogate the treaty, annex it to the Company's dominions and send the Nawab into exile. A vivid pictorial history of the times has been created by Satyajit Ray in his path-breaking film, *Shatranj ke Khiladi* (The Chess Players), based on a story by Munshi Prem Chand. This film accurately depicts the socio-cultural mores of mid-nineteenth century. It also features Pandit Birju Maharaj in a cameo as the *thumri* singer in the Nawab's court, singing in his own voice, and the versatile actor Amjad Khan in the role of the Nawab singing, also in his own voice, snatches of Wajid Ali's original poetry. The lowly status of the *tabalchi*, as described in the Introduction, has also been accurately depicted by the master film maker, who had an unfailing eye for historical detail.

Wajid Ali Shah was exiled to Calcutta, where he was allotted a large estate called *Metia Burj*, on the outskirts of the city. The Nawab was accompanied into exile by an endless retinue of wives, concubines, cooks, and most importantly, highly skilled singers, musicians, and dancing girls. Though guilty of misgoverning his kingdom on a scandalous scale, the Nawab was, nonetheless, a great connoisseur of art and culture. A gifted kathak dancer, singer, and poet himself, he has a number of *thumris* to his credit, penned under his *nom de plume*, Akhtar Pia. His most famous *thumri*, *Baabul mora naihar chhooto hi jaaye* was composed in raga Bhairavi. It has been recorded by many singers, most notably K.L. Saigal in the 1930s film, *Street Singer*. The massive entourage which accompanied him into exile was to form the nucleus of the artistic and social life of cosmopolitan Calcutta in the days to come. At the time of his exile, Wajid Ali

Shah was thirty-four years old. He lived in for another thirty years in Calcutta before passing away in 1887. It was during this period that Calcutta became a centre of classical music and dance (kathak), the after effects of which lasted upto the first quarter of the twentieth century.

GROWTH OF HINDUSTANI CLASSICAL MUSIC IN CALCUTTA

From about 1860 onwards, Calcutta became the foremost hub of Hindustani classical music in India, a position which it retained for a hundred years before yielding it to Bombay. Right from the battle of Plassey in 1757, the British East India Company had ruled Bengal through its wealthy, landowning zamindars, who, over the years, became indolent and financially dependant on local moneylenders to support their luxurious lifestyles. After the arrival of Wajid Ali Shah and his court-in-exile, both the zamindars and their financiers became generous patrons of the musicians, singers and dancers, around whom the city's artistic life began to revolve. When the Indian film and music recording companies finally came into being, Calcutta was their natural choice to set up shop. Moreover, many famous musicians of the time had their origins in the courts of local rajas and zamindars, where they, their descendants and their gharanas prospered and polished their craft to perfection. The Imdaad khani gharana of the sitar/surbahar, renowned for its elegant style of playing in the *gayaki ang*, has its origins in Bengal, where Ustad Imdaad Khan was a musician in the durbar of the Raja of Gauripur. Ustad Ali Akbar Khan, the doyen of sarod (being a Bengali), also based himself in Calcutta later, as did Ustad Bade Ghulam Ali Khan and Ustad Amir Khan in the 1960s and

70s (though both were non-Bengalis), due to the conducive ambiance the city provided for artistes of all hues. Though Calcutta was never associated with any gharana of music, many eminent musicians of various schools gravitated to it as a result of the historical developments of the time. Prithviraj Kapoor and Ashok Kumar; K.L. Saigal, and Talat Mehmood, the famous ghazal maestro, all started their careers there, as did the legendary showman, Raj Kapoor.

Renowned poet and novelist Sunil Gangopadhyay's award winning book, *Those Days*, gives an engrossing account, in the historical fiction style, of the socio-political, cultural, and artistic life of Calcutta in the nineteenth century. Nawab Wajid Ali Shah's forced abdication and exile were followed by the the social degradation of Indian music and dance at the hands of its British overlords, whose capital Calcutta was at the time. British historian William Dalrymple also has a thing or two to say about this denigratory attitude of the Imperialists towards the cultural practices of the Indians in his book, *The Last Mughal*. It is worth mentioning that ITC Sangeet Research Academy, run by the corporate house ITC Ltd, is also located in Calcutta (now Kolkata). It was established in 1978 with Pandit Vijay Kichlu of the classical vocal duo, Kichlu Brothers as its founding director. Over the years, it has trained many talented youngsters in the *guru-shishya parampara*. Among its famous alumni are Rashid Khan and Ajoy Chakraborty, and the latter's daughter, Kaushiki Chakrabarty Desikan.

EVOLUTION AND DEVELOPMENT OF THE SAROD

It is not so well known that what we see today as the sarod, was actually developed in Calcutta over the years. It had passed through many avatars earlier, before it was born in its present one. There was the Afghan/Central Asian *Rabab*, the *Dhrupadi Rabab* (also called the *Rudra Veena* and *Been*), then the *Sur Shringar* (also called the *Sur Rabab*). While the earlier versions had a wooden finger board, by the early 20th century, a metallic, fretless finger board had been developed. The present sarod owes a great deal to Pandit Radhika Mohan Moitra/Maitreya (1917-81) and his contemporary, Ustad (Baba) Allahuddin Khan, the latter being senior, both of whom lived and worked in Calcutta. This is a separate subject, which aspiring *rasiks* can read about on their own.

BAIJI-S AND THE KOTHA TRADITION

Forced out from the palaces of the aristocracy, dancers, singers, and their accompanists were herded into *kothas* or dancing houses, where they continued to entertain the elite. Many discerning *rasiks* became frequent visitors to these *kothas*, where singers and dancers of acknowledged artistic merit kept the art alive. *Kothas* originated in Wajid Ali Shah's Awadh and moved with him to Calcutta in 1856-7. Muzaffar Ali's award winning film, *Umrao Jaan* (1981) gives a true and vivid account of *kotha* culture. His highly stylized film direction is matched, if not surpassed, by music director Khayyam's compositions which constitute one of the finest scores in the canon of Hindi film music. The courtesans hosting these *kothas* were known as *Baiji-s* and were high-class music professionals, contrary to the belief that they were no more than glorified courtesans. Present generations should know that it was these *baiji-s* that kept this vital aspect of Hindustani culture alive during its lean period during British rule. Perhaps the most famous *baiji* of the time was Gauhar Jaan. A Eurasian of Armenian descent, she was renowned for her knowledge and skills in *khayal* and *thumri* gayaki. She signifies the last stage of the dying *kotha* tradition in Calcutta and the first of its nascent recording industry, thereby providing a vital link between the two. Gauhar Jaan became the first studio recording artiste in India, when she recorded a short khayal *bandish* in raga *Jogiya* on a 78 rpm record in 1902. It was these *kothas* that provided early recruits to studios of the budding film industry, singers, dancers, and instrumentalists alike. In the course of time, as the film and recording industry took root, talented *kothewaalis* began to move out of their *kothas*, and into the freedom of films and recording studios. Their old *kothas* were soon reduced to a shadow of their former glory, bringing to an end a glorious era. The first cinema hall in India, Elphinstone Picture Palace, was also established in Calcutta by J.F. Madan in 1907.

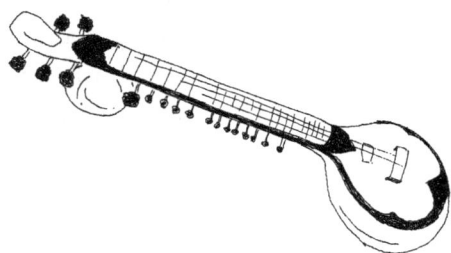

18

Hindustani Raga Sangeet in Hindi Films

On 8 Febtuary 2012, the 71st birth anniversary of late ghazal maestro, Jagjit Singh was observed in Mumbai (six months after his sad demise). He was a very popular man, given to forging easy friendships and was also known for his ready sense of humour and his encouragement of young talent. He had lived a joyous life and when he passed away, left behind a multitude of friends and admirers, hundreds of whom came from far and near to participate in the musical programme arranged to celebrate the occasion. The hall was choc-a-bloc with the who's who of the film and music industry. Ustad Ghulam Ali, the famous ghazal singer from Pakistan was there to sing, as were Anup Jalota, Talat Aziz (whose career Jagjit had launched in the 1990s), Sonu Nigam, Hariharan, Shaan and the master of Carnatic and world music, Dr L Subramanium and his singer wife, Suchitra Krishnamurthy (both of whom presented a riveting violin and vocal duet.) Pandit Jasraj, Ustad Ghulam Mustafa Khan, Yash Chopra, Javed Akhtar, Shabana Azmi and many other actors, poets, singers and music composers were among the audience.

Among all the items presented, the one that brought the house down was by a singer of pure classical music. Ustad

Rashid Khan, an alumnus of the ITC Sangeet Research Academy, Kolkata who is also one of the most sought after classical vocalists today, sang Ustad Bade Ghulam Ali Khan's original and immortal *thumri* in raga *Punjabi Maand*, *'Yaad piya ki aaye'* (though Rashid Khan sang it in a slightly variant raga, *Bhinna Khadaj*.) Listeners gave him a long, resounding and well deserved standing ovation and his performance will long be remembered by country wide TV watchers who saw the show.

Jagjit Singh signifies the midway point between raga sangeet and popular (film as well as non-film) music. Here was a man thoroughly trained in the classical tradition, who used all the ornamental techniques *(alankaar)* of raga sangeet to embellish his music, yet ensured that it remained outside the classical fold. It was this apparent paradox that endeared him to lay people who rushed in droves to his concerts because he had simplified the style generally associated with traditional ghazal gayaki and contemporized it with modern day popular music. The confluence of young and old talents of the film music fraternity at the birth centenary of a semi-classical singer-composer and the standing ovation they jointly gave to a practitioner of pure raga sangeet is indicative of the close, though unacknowledged, links between all three genres: film, classical and semi-classical music.

THE CLASSICAL LEGACY

Ever since the Hindi sound film industry came into being with its first release, *Alam Ara* in 1931, classical music has been the mainstay of its music. In the early days, it was used more in its natural form as Raga Sangeet itself, as in the 1952 film,

Baiju Bawra. As time passed, new and more innovative music directors joined the industry who began composing songs not as Raga *bandishes*, but as raga-based, popular songs. This trend has remained in place ever since and the majority of film song compositions even now (except for imitative, pseudo-westernised 'pop' or 'rock') continue to be based on classical ragas. Raga sangeet is a contemplative, mood intensive (*Bhaav pradhaan*) music. This *ras-bhava* is carried on the pattern of notes of the raga on which the song is based. Other than this pattern of notes, the film song may contain none of the other qualities that personify the raga in its original *bandish*, such as tabla accompaniment, layakari and taankari etc. Yet, the *ras-bhava* is retained in the film song even it is accompanied by Western instruments like the piano, violins and drums.

The legacy of our classical music weighs so heavily on our culture that it is impossible to ignore its effects on our musical creativity. All our folk songs are actually *deshi* ragas in their raw form, which were taken up by pundits and refined to the level of *shastriya* sangeet over time. Every permutation and combination of the twelve notes of the musical scale has already been conceived over the centuries. Thus, whenever a composer sits down with his Harmonium to compose, he unwittingly hits upon a combination of notes that already exists, either as in its *deshi* form, or as a *maargi* raga composed by some learned pundit long ago. There is no escape from it, except to jettison the legacy altogether and create, what Dilip Kumar calls 'orchestrated noise.' It is not very well known that the great thespian mentioned above is also a gifted singer himself, well versed in the classical tradition. He sang a beautiful *thumri* duet with Lata Mangeshkar for

Hrishikesh Mukherji's first directorial venture in 1957, *Musafir* (music by Salil Chaudhuri) in which he had a small role as a guest artiste. The song is *'Laagi naahi chhoote Raama, chaahe jiya jaaye.'*

These facts were acknowledged right from the start by Hindi film music composers, all of whom were thoroughly well versed in our classical legacy. They freely and unabashedly used classical ragas to base their compositions on. There was no concept of anyone holding copyrights of these ragas and the melodies thus composed, coupled with the lyrics of renowned poets like Kaifi Azmi, Shailendra and Shakeel Badayuni became a staple of the film industry. Over the decades, hundreds and thousands of film songs have been composed based on classical music ragas. It is unlikely that this will ever cease, regardless of the new multiplex culture pervading the film industry, a section of which is catering to metro audiences with new age films in the realist genre. The big boys will always make films with music as hithertofore, like *My name is Khan, Fanaa, Guru* and *Rockstar*, the songs of which were runaway hits due to the raga heritage from which they were born.

FAMOUS CLASSICAL MUSICIANS IN HINDI FILMS

Among the earliest films to have used classical singers is *Baiju Bawra* (1952) in which the great singers, Ustad Amir Khan and Pundit DV Paluskar both sang four songs under Naushad's baton. Another film (which was the story of a shehnai player) *Goonj uthi Shehnai* (1959) featured the shehnai of Ustad Bismillah Khan throughout the film, as well as an instrumental *jugalbandi* with the highly talented and innovative sitarist, Ustad Abdul Halim Jaffar Khan. The

music director was Vasant Desi. Other singers who have sung
for films are the *jugalbandi* brothers, Pandits Rajan and Sajan
Mishra of the Benaras gharana in the film *Sur Sangam* (1985),
starring Girish Karnad and Jaya Prada in which the brothers
sang eight songs, singly, together and with other singers like
Lata Mangeshkar and Anuradha Paudhwal, under the music
direction of Lakshmikant-Pyarelal. In Hrishikesh Mukherji's
award winning film, *Anuradha* featuring Balraj Sahni and
Leela Naidu, the music direction was provided by Pandit
Ravi Shankar. These are only a few instances. An archivist
would be able to give many more.

The most famous film, K. Asif's *Mughal-e Azam* featured
the great singer, Ustad Bade Ghulam Ali Khan in which he
sang two songs under the music direction of Naushad. The
first was raga *Ragaeshri* based *'Shubh din aayo, raj dulara'*
which is sung in the backdrop of the long drawn sequence
of Salim's return to the palace after a decade of exile-cum-
battlefield training. The second is sung during the scene
which Mahesh Bhatt has called the most erotic in the history
of Hindi cinema. This is the night long tryst between Salim
and Anarkali under a flower laden tree, Miyan Tansen shown
in silhouette, singing in the background, as the two make love
without bodily contact: only the Prince caressing Anarkali's
face with a heron plume. This was the Ustad's rendition of
a *thumri* in raga *Sohini, 'Prem jogan ban ke'* which remains the
finest example of the coming together of the film and classical
music worlds. Any aesthetic film goer with a musical ear will
agree with Mahesh Bhatt's opinion, so soul stirring is the
Ustad's voice, so scorching the chemistry between the pair of
lovers/actors and so exquisite the cinematography.

RAGA SANGEET AND FILM MUSIC: AN UNACKNOWLEDGED BOND
It is well known that when films first began to be made
in India, the profession was held in very low esteem in
society. When Dada Saheb Phalke was making his first film,
Harishchandra, he had to keep it and the film studio a secret
from the world by telling everyone that he was running a
'factory' and the actors and film technicians were factory
workers. Except for a few established film families of the
1940s like the Kapoors, the Shantarams, Himanshu Rai and
Devika Rani, etc, respectable men and women hesitated to
join, fearing social ostracism if they ventured into the budding
industry. Consequently, the stalwarts of the classical music
fraternity also looked down on the industry and refused to
sing for films. Ustad Bade Ghulam Ali famously tried to fob
off K. Asif when the latter approached with a request to
sing for *Mughal-e-Azam*, by asking for the then (mid-1950s)
exhorbitant fee of Rs 25,000. It was only due to Naushad's
intervention that the Ustad finally relented, though he also
exacted his quoted fee, considered the highest ever paid to
a singer till then. This was in marked contrast to the high
regard and esteem in which film musicians and singers held
the classicists. It was only when the Golden Age of film
music got well underway in the mid-1970s that the classical
fraternity acknowledged the fact that great film music
composers of the day like S.D. Burman, Madan Mohan,
Roshan, Khayyam and Salil Choudhury were really doing
a remarkable job. They grudgingly accepted that these
composers were indeed producing mavellous, raga-based
film songs, replete with all the *ras-bhava* of raga sangeet,
and that too, only in the short span of three minutes that

the 78 rpm format permitted. This fact is now universally acknowleged by classicists, connoisseurs and *rasiks* alike.

SOME MEMORABLE RAGA-BASED HINDI FILM SONGS

As mentioned earlier, a raga-based film song may be presented in any form: In its original mould as a full fledged *bandish* like the raga *Hamir* based song *'Madhuban mein Radhika naache re'* from the film *Kohinoor*/1960 (music by Naushad) which remains popular on TV programmes like Chitrahar over half a century later; or in a completely different avatar as a glamourous, Westernised dance sequence like *'Chura liya hai tumne jo dil ko'* sung on screen by a skirt clad Zeenat Aman swaying gracefully, guitar in hand, in the film *Yaadon ki baaraat* (music by R.D. Burman.) This song is based on raga *Piloo*. Some well known and much loved, popular film songs are listed below, with the name of the raga they are based on and the name of their composer:

'Dost Dost naa raha, pyaar pyaar naa raha' from the film Sangam *(music by Shankar-Jaikishan) based on raga Bhairavi.*

'Do hanson ka joda, bichhad gayo re, gajab bhayo Rama julam bhayo re' from the film Ganga Jamuna *(music by Naushad) based on raga Bhairavi.*

'Yeh kyaa jagah hai doston, yeh kaunsa dayaar hai' from the film Umrao Jaan *(music by Khayyam) based on raga Behag.*

'Main to ek khwaab hoon, is khwaab se tu pyaar na kar' from the film Himalaya ki Gode Mein *(music by Kalyanji-Anandji) based on raga Todi.*

'Dil hoom hoom karey' from the film Rudaali *(music by Bhupen Hazarika) based on raga Bhopali (known as raga Mohanan in Carnatic sangeet.)*

'Kabhi khud pe, kabhi haalaat pe rona aaya' from the film Hum Dono *(music by Jaidev) based on raga Gara.*

'Mere mehboob, tujhe meri mohabbat ki qasam' from the film Mere Mehboob *(music by Naushad) based on raga Jhinjhoti*

'Jaayein to jaayein kahaan, samajhe gaa kaun yahaan' from the film Taxi Driver *(music by S.D. Burman) based on raga Jogiya.*

'Inhi logon ne, inhi logon ne le liya dupatta mera' from the film Pakeeza *(music by Ghulam Ahmed/Naushad) based on raga Yaman Kalyan.*

'Kahin deep jaley kahin dil' from the film Bees Saal Baad *(music by Hemant Kumar) based on raga Shiv Ranjini.*

'Breathless' Non-film song written by Javed Akhtar and sung by *Shankar Mahadevan under the music direction of Shankar-Ehsaan-Loy, based on raga Yaman Kalyan.*

'Kuchh to loge kahenge, logon ka kaam hai kehna' from the film Amar Prem *(music by RD Burman) based on raga Khamaaj.*

'Main pyaar ka raahi hoon, teri zulf ke saaye mein' from the film Ek Musafir ek Haseena *(music by O.P. Nayyar) based on raga Kirwani.*

'Neela aasmaan so gaya' from the film Silsila, *famously sung by superstar Amitabh Bachchan in his own voice (music by Shiv-Hari) based on raga Pahadi.*

'Kaise din beete re, kaise beeti ratiyaan, piya jaane naa' from the film Anuradha *(music by Pandit Ravi Shankar) based on raga Maanj Khamaaj.*

19

The Future of Hindustani Classical Music

Every music conference, seminar, or symposium in the last quarter of a century has ended up drawing the following conclusion: 'The future of Hindustani Classical Music is safe and, despite a rapidly changing world, its continued wellbeing is assured in the hands of coming generations.' These groups of highly respected individuals of proven talent and erudition, however, appear to remain oblivious of contrary winds blowing in the face of such a rosy conclusion. There is also a tendency of brushing aside contradicting views as being those of crass materialists who do not care for this ancient art, but seek to dilute its timeless spiritual core for commercial gain.

Traditionalists who believe that Hindustani classical music is destined to stay safe and sound as hithertofore, have never really sought out the considered views of sincere and talented youngsters among their own fraternity, who may be able to offer an alternative to the present format which has remained more or less unchanged for almost a century. No one has really asked for the views of 'the coming generations' of artistes and *rasiks*, into whose hands the future is being so trustingly entrusted. Many young, gifted musicians and knowledgeable listeners alike, thus simply hold their peace, leaving their opinions unspoken for fear of upsetting their revered gurus, whom they genuinely respect and sincerely admire for the long and arduous journey they have survived to reach the pinnacle of their artistic accomplishments.

I have been going to Hindustani classical music concerts half my life. Earlier, there used to be a large percentage of young *rasiks* among the audience, thronging live performances that stretched far into the night. These days, when one goes to concerts at the old, familiar haunts in Calcutta, Poona, and Bombay (now Kolkata, Pune, and Mumbai, respectively), one sees few young people among the audience. I distinctly recall young college boys and girls, who could barely afford the balcony tickets at Kalamandir in Calcutta in the 1960s and 70s, calling out to famous artistes like the late Ustads Amir Khan or Ali Akbar Khan (who were themselves in their forties then) with requests for *Pooriya Dhanashri, Darbari Kanhada,* or some other favourite raga. The Ustads always smiled, gladly heeded the calls, and readily obliged their young audiences. The absence of such youthful participation now may lead us to conclude that Hindustani classical music is losing its popularity among the young. Yet, this could be a gravely mistaken conclusion which, if true, makes it hard to explain why classical music albums continue to sell briskly and youngsters, in large numbers, continue to enter the field as professional musicians. I have visited some music stores, both big and small, to gauge the sales trends of Hindustani classical music albums. In Pune and Mumbai, the sales of vocal raga sangeet albums is brisk, specially among serious listeners. In Kolkata, where I live, the popularity of vocal and instrumental albums is almost equal, with sitar, sarod, flute, and santoor dominating. In all three cities, it is the younger generation of local Marathis and Bengalis who are the most avid buyers. In all three places, lounge music was the preferred listening choice among 'metropolitan' listeners. Besides *sitarist* Purbayan Chatterji and vocalist Arshad Ali, some other upcoming musicians are Vikas Bharadwaj (sitar), Kumar Mukherjee and Pushkar Lele (both vocal.)

On balance, we can realistically arrive at the following conclusions: Music lovers have remained at a constant level, but audiences at live performances, particularly the young among them, have declined. The number of listeners of recorded music is growing, who wish to listen to the music of their choice, for durations that they please and at a time and place of their choosing. Similarly, the growing number of talented youngsters entering the field as professional artistes is also a healthy sign. Top class artistes have fewer but better attended live concerts, which are being increasingly restricted to the metropolitan cities of India. Performances of live concerts abroad, on the other hand, have shown a marked increase. Earlier, the usual venues were New York, Los Angeles, London and Paris. These have now increased to include Eastern Europe, Japan, and Australia as well, which also accounts for the long duration our musicians spend abroad as well the growing sale of their CDs globally.

WINDS OF CHANGE

Change is inevitable, no matter how long it takes in coming. We have discussed the many changes that took place in Hindustani Classical music in the course of its evolution from ancient Vedic chants of the second century BCE to the present day. Change is, therefore, bound to come again. How and when this will happen, is the question to which we seek answers today. An ancient and time-honoured tradition can only be questioned by someone who himself holds a position of honour in that tradition.

Manna Dey is one such person. A highly gifted and versatile singer, he has made a name for himself in every field, including classical music (particularly in raga-based film songs) for over half a century. Pundits of every persuasion are unanimous in their admiration of his many and varied achievements. In September 2009, at the venerable age of ninety, he was honoured with the Dada Saheb Phalke Award for his lifetime achievements in Indian films. In an interview to The Times of India, Kolkata dated 4 October 2009 on the twin occasions of the award and his ninetieth birthday, he unequivocally made known his disregard for the way in which classical music is practiced and presented to audiences today.

It should be a matter of concern to music lovers in general and the classical music fraternity in particular, that a singer of such consummate skill and so well versed in the classics should hold the current format of classical music recitals in such low esteem. When asked if he had ever thought of pursuing a career in Hindustani classical music, the classically trained singer replied firmly in the negative, terming the current format of recitals 'repetitive and boring'. Though he speaks perfect English and Hindi, he chose his mother tongue, Bengali, to drive home the point: *'Raga chhire jae oibhabe taante taante'* (They go on and on, ripping the raga to shreds). To a second question about the new trend towards short duration, live music recitals, he gave his approval, calling it a 'healthy sign.'

Another example of the winds of change is that of a producer of highly popular TV music shows which have been watched widely throughout the length and breadth of India. Though neither as venerated (so far) nor honoured as Manna Dey and less that half his age, Gajendra Singh has been producing music (singing) talent competitions like *Saregama* for TV, in which great personalities like Lata Mangeshkar, Pandit Ravi Shankar, and famous film music directors like Khayyam and O.P. Nayyar have participated as judges and chief guests. Viewer rating (though not an indicator of the merit of a TV programme) of his shows has reached record breaking heights. Interestingly, among the best talents he unearthed, the majority had received classical training and many of them presented raga-based compositions as their prize winning performances.

When he was interviewed on Doordarshan on 21 September 2009, Gajendra Singh first made his deep respect for raga sangeet in general and his high regard for its practitioners in particular, perfectly clear. Thereafter, he opened up about the serious shortcomings in the current format of Hindustani classical music, which prevented music producers like him from presenting it on TV shows. (Though we know that raga sangeet is not a popular music genre, it is worth exploring ways and means by which it can be presented on popular TV programmes, possibly in an altered format). In his view, the current format of khayal recitals appears as if the artiste was going through his daily *riyaaz* (practice), repeating musical phrases again and again, doing voice modulation excercises, practicing scales and going on for hours, thus making it unsuitable for telecasting (see Manna Dey's comments in

Bengali given in the first example above). Without elaborating further, he left it to the viewer to judge what shape Hindustani classical music recitals should take if they are to retain audience interest, even among informed listeners.

As discussed, pure classical music encompasses both, vocal khayal gayaki and instrumental recitals in the Khayal style. This genre and its semi-classical counterparts like *thumri* and *∂aa∂ra* all together comprise what is now called raga sangeet. It is clear that what Manna Dey and Gajendra Singh called 'boring and repetitive' was a reference to the first type, i.e. khayal gayaki and khayal style instrumental recitals. Two random and conflicting thoughts on the issues raised by Manna Dey and Gajendra Singh come to mind.

Raga Sangeet is a 'mood music' wherein a raga, by its pattern of notes and their sequence of use, seeks to evoke its ruling mood-emotion (*ra∂-bhava*). This is evoked and its dominant mood-emotion, fully aroused when the performer deliniates its pattern of notes (including its all important *paka∂*) in detail and at length, as explained in the chapter 'Concert and Recital'. This is achieved primarily by the *alap* and the *vilambit* khayal, both of which may last thirty minutes each. In other words, setting the mood requires time. Contrary to this, we also know that at one time or another during their long careers, the best musicians in the last half a century have recorded ten to fifteen short *bandi∂h*es on a single album, all of which have all gone on to achieve tremendous, everlasting popularity. (In any case, during the days of 78 rpm records, the songs lasted only three-and-a-half minutes). Details of short duration recordings are given in the chapter entitled 'Recommended Progress: In Stages and by Genres'.

We have discussed both sides of the coin: On one side, the format in which Hindustani classical music recitals have been presented over the last century and on the other, the views of two individuals who have a deep involvement in music, one ninety years old and the other, half his age. Similarly, we have noted the views of pundits who feel that the future of raga sangeet is secure, even though we see fewer young people at live concerts. Conversely, talented youngsters continue to enter the field as professional musicians while the sale of recorded albums continues unabated. Live concerts in India are fewer but better attended, whereas they are growing in number over the rest of the world, reaching more countries than ever before. What the future holds, only time will tell. It is for the musicians and musicologists to decide what the format of Hindustani classical music recitals in the future should be, if this magnificent genre is to retain its pride of place in the classical arts of India and the world.

Bibliography and Recommended Reading

Ali, Amaan & Ayaan Ali, *50 Maestros, 50 Recordings*, Harper Collins, Delhi, 2009.

Basham, A.L., *The Wonder that was India*, Rupa & Co., Delhi, 1981.

Chakraborty, Ajoy, *Shrutinandan*, Macmillan India Ltd, Kolkata, 2002.

Devidayal, Namita, *The Music Room*, Random House India, Delhi, 2008.

Gilani, Malti & Quratulain Hyder, *Ustad Bade Ghulam Ali Khan 'Sabrang, his Life and Music*, Harman Publishing House, New Delhi, 2003.

Holroyde, Peggy, *The Music of India*, Praeger Publishers, New York and Washington, 1972.

'Khayal Gharanas' (ITC Sangeet Research Academy, Kolkata, 2004): ITC Sangeet Research Academy; 1, N.S.C. Bose Road, Kolkata.

Mukherji, Kumar Prasad, *The Lost World of Hindustani Music*, Penguin Books India, Delhi, 2006.

Pandit Amarnath, *Living Idioms in Hindustani Music*, Vikas Publishing House, Delhi, 1989.

Pingle, Bh. A., *Indian Music*, (Kathiawar, 1898), Indian Books Centre, Delhi, reprinted 1989.

Rahamin, Atiya Begum Fyzee, *The Music of India*, (first published in 1925), Low Priced Publications, Delhi, reprinted 1990.

Rosenthal, Ethel, *The Story of Indian Music and its Instruments,* Low Price Publications, Delhi, reprinted 1990.

NOTES

1. *The Music of India* by Peggy Holroyde, Foreword by Pt. Ravi Shankar (Praeger Publishers, New York, 1972).

2. Dr Narayana Menon - Quoted by Peggy Holroyde (ibid.)

3. O. Goswami from his book, *The Story of Indian Music* (Asia Publishing House, London, 1959).

4. From an article entitled 'My House, My Song' by Renuka Narayana.

5. *Shrutinandan* by Ajoy Chakraborty (Macmillan India Ltd. Kolkata, 2002).

6. 'Crossroads', a panel discussion and participatory seminar held at the ITC Sangeet Research Academy, Kolkata.

Index

About the Author

Vijay Prakash Singha studied at Mayo College, Ajmer and Rajasthan University, Jaipur before joining the Indian Military Academy, Dehradun in 1967. He got infatuated with Hindustani classical music in his teens, and was able to indulge in it throughout his career postings all over India. This guidebook is an effort to share his passion with others. He now lives in Kolkata with his wife and continues to enjoy the best of the new generation of artistes.